A HISTORY *of* WESTERN ART

Bernini's David *(1623),
depicted in the
moment before
his slingshot throw.
See page 68.*

Library of Congress Cataloging-in-Publication Data:

Mason, Antony.
A history of Western art : from prehistory to the 20th century / by Antony
Mason ; edited by John T. Spike.
p. cm.
Includes index.
ISBN-13: 978-0-8109-9421-8 (hardcover with jacket)
ISBN-10: 0-8109-9421-6 (hardcover with jacket)
1. Art—History. I. Spike, John T. II. Title.

N5300.M315 2007
709—dc22

Copyright © 2007 McRae Books Srl, Florence (Italy)

A History of Western Art
was created and produced by McRae Books
Via del Salviatino, 1 – Fiesole (Florence) Italy
info@mcraebooks.com
www.mcraebooks.com

SERIES EDITOR Anne McRae
TEXT Antony Mason
EDITED BY John T. Spike
LAYOUTS Nick Leggett (Starry Dog Books ltd)

ART DIRECTOR Marco Nardi
EDITING Loredana Agosta
REPRO Raf, Florence (Italy)
PICTURE RESEARCH Loredana Agosta

Printed and bound in China by L-Rex Printing, Hong Kong

10 9 8 7 6 5 4 3 2 1

HNA
harry n. abrams, inc.
a subsidiary of La Martinière Groupe
115 West 18th Street
New York, NY 10011
www.hnabooks.com

A HISTORY *of* WESTERN ART

From Prehistory to the 20th Century

ANTONY MASON Edited by JOHN T. SPIKE

Abrams Books for Young Readers
New York

Contents

Introduction

There are 30,000 years of history in Western Art. Even before the remotest signs of civilization appeared, human beings were fashioning sculptures and painting images of animals on the walls of caves with extraordinarily deft artistic skills. For centuries, it seemed that the artist's goal was to create a perfect likeness of the world we see around us. But there was always more to art than imitation. It was a way of making a statement about the world, commenting on the nature of human existence, and expressing profound emotion. Over the last 150 years or so, with an accelerating pace, the history of art has shown there are many ways to do this, and now the options for artists have been thrown wide open. This book provides an accessible and stimulating overview of the story of art in the West, from its origins right up to the present day.

Above: A picture from a tomb wall, dating to around 1350 BCE. p11

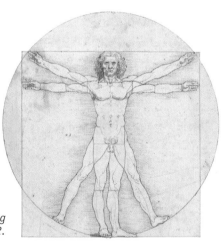

Right: Leonardo's drawing of The Vitruvian Man *as on page 52.*

Below: Pollock dripped, dribbled, splashed, and slopped paint straight from the tin. p119

PREHISTORIC MATERIALS

The world's first artists worked with the natural materials that they found around them. Iron oxide (hematite or ochre) produced red; by heating it in a fire, it could produce various pigments, or colors, ranging from yellow to purple. Charcoal (from burnt wood) made black. Lumps of such materials could be used to draw outlines, or they could be crushed into a powder, then mixed with water and perhaps animal fat to produce paint. Flat stones, or flat bones such as shoulder blades, served as palettes. Sharp, hard stones could be used to engrave lines in the softer surfaces of cave walls. Brushes were made from animal fur or bristles, feathers, or moss, or by chewing on sticks or reeds to separate out the fibers. But often the artists simply applied the paint with their fingers, or they used a stencil technique by blowing mouthfuls of paint in a fine mist over a shape, such as their own hand.

Right: This stone was found in a cave in South Africa inhabited about 3 million years ago by Australopithecines, possible ancestors of modern human beings. They may have treasured it because it resembles a human face—a very early example of artistic selection.

Left: Early artists made pigment by crushing naturally occurring minerals and charcoal.

Prehistoric Art

Human beings clearly have a natural instinct to create art. It is one of the characteristics of humans that set them apart from almost all other animal species. The earliest paintings, preserved deep inside caves, were created as long ago as 30,000 BCE, and the earliest known fully carved sculptures date to roughly the same period. This was a time when people lived by hunting animals and gathering wild food, moving from place to place to follow the herds and the seasons. They lived in temporary shelters made of timber and skins, and sometimes in rock shelters and caves. Their tools were made of stone, wood, bone, and horn. We call this the Stone Age—the age before any metals were used. During the Neolithic period (New Stone Age), beginning in about 10,000 BCE, people began to farm and lead more settled lives in villages. This happened first in the Middle East, then spread into Europe gradually between about 6000 and 4000 BCE.

Magic and Ritual

No one knows for certain what inspired the first artists to draw and paint and sculpt. A constant concern was finding food: For Stone Age people, armed just with handmade bows and spears tipped with flint heads, hunting was never easy. It was possible that animal pictures were created as parts of rituals or ceremonies of magic designed to help hunters. Some surviving paintings are deep inside caves, where they could be seen only in the light of flaming torches, fires, or lamps burning animal fat, so it is unlikely that they were made simply for decoration.

Below: A painting in a cave at Valtorta, Spain, shows figures using bows and arrows to hunt deer. In prehistoric painting, humans usually appear only as sketchy stick figures like these.

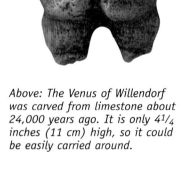

Above: The Venus of Willendorf was carved from limestone about 24,000 years ago. It is only 4$\frac{1}{4}$ inches (11 cm) high, so it could be easily carried around.

Sculpture

It is likely that the first stone sculptures were made from rocks that were already shaped in a way that suggested other forms. Small, carved figures of naked women have been found across Europe; they are thought to have been fertility symbols, and are called Venus figures, after the Roman goddess of love. Some were carved from soft limestone, others from ivory (mammoth tusk), and others were molded from clay and hardened by fire.

Left: A picture in the cave of Trois Frères in Ariège, France, seems to depict a man dressed in a deer skin, perhaps performing a magic hunting ritual. It has been named The Sorcerer.

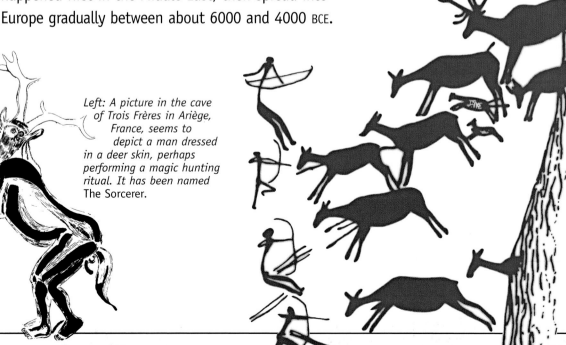

SHOWCASE: CAVE PAINTING AT LASCAUX

One of the world's most famous sets of prehistoric cave paintings is at Lascaux, in the Dordogne region of France. Dating to around 17,000 BCE, it contains almost 600 animals, depicted with extraordinary skill and vitality. The cave was discovered by accident by four teenagers in 1940. Because exposure to air has damaged the paintings, the cave is now closed to the public, but a full-size replica has been made nearby. The paintings shown here come from the part of the cave known as the Great Hall of the Bulls.

Horses are shown running alongside the bulls. A sense of scale does not seem to have mattered to the artists.

The bulls are aurochs, a kind of cattle that is now extinct.

The colors were made from charcoal, ochre, and manganese oxide (black).

Standing Stones and Monuments
During the Neolithic period, massive stone monuments were built at various places across Europe. Many of them consist of huge, long stones (megaliths) placed vertically in the ground and arranged in avenues or in circles. Some (like Stonehenge, below) have crosspieces, forming primitive arches—a wonder of engineering, given the huge weight of the stones. Dolmens have three or more large stones roofed with a capstone. Single standing stones, called menhirs, were sometimes carved with shallow relief images. Some of these great stone monuments were burial grounds, but the purpose of many remains a mystery. They may have been temples, or some kind of observatories that marked the movement of the sun and stars, and the change of seasons— which was important for farming.

Right: A sandstone menhir from Saint-Sernins-sur-Rance, France, has been carved with an expressive image of a human figure. It dates from about 3500 BCE.

Below right: An aerial view of Stonehenge shows the outer, older rings of earth banks, created in about 3100 BCE. The earliest monument here may have been built of timber posts.

Ancient Near East

Sumer

The very first Mesopotamian civilization was called Sumer, which developed around 3500 BCE and lasted for about 1,500 years. It consisted of about 50 city-states—cities that behaved like independent mini-nations. The most important were at Eridu, Uruk, and Ur. The royal cemetery at Ur was excavated in 1926–32, and the tomb of "Queen" Pu-Abi was found to contain some of the most splendid treasures of the ancient world, including delicate gold jewelry, musical instruments, and sculpture. The Sumerians developed the world's earliest form of writing. It is called cuneiform, meaning "wedge-shaped," because it was written by pressing the wedge-shaped tip of a reed into tablets of damp clay to form the characters.

The history of civilization is closely related to the development of cities. Farming, and a secure supply of food, allowed people to settle in villages; villages grew into towns, and towns into cities. Cities became centers of power, religion, and culture. City dwellers no longer had to farm: They could earn their living through trade as merchants, or by pursuing a craft, such as pottery or carpentry. Artists also worked in cities, because there were plenty of wealthy people— royalty, nobles, and religious authorities—who would pay for their work. Some of the world's first cities developed in the Near East, particularly in Mesopotamia, the area now occupied mainly by Iraq. By about 3500 BCE, the Near East had begun to enter the Bronze Age: The discovery of bronze, an alloy of copper and tin, provided the means to make stronger and sharper tools.

Above: This bronze head of an Akkadian ruler dates to about 2300–2200 BCE, and may be a portrait of King Sargon.

Ziggurats

The ancient Mesopotamians built colossal stepped monuments called ziggurats. Long ramps or staircases led up the sides to reach flat platforms on the top, where shrines to the gods were built. These huge structures were made of a solid core of mud brick (clay bricks baked hard in the sun), with kiln-fired bricks— sometimes glazed—on the outside. It is thought that the story of the Tower of Babel, from the Old Testament of the Bible, might be based on a ziggurat.

Akkad

Akkad was a city-state in central Mesopotamia. Under King Sargon I (reigned c. 2340–2305 BCE), Akkad conquered Sumer and ruled over it for about 150 years. The city of Akkad has never been found, but it was perhaps located at the city known as Sippar, or faced it across the Euphrates River. The Akkadians were skilled artists, producing delicate stone relief carvings (telling the story of Akkadian conquests) and sculpture made of cast bronze and gold. They also produced clay statuettes of nude female figures, thought to be religious idols. The Akkadians wrote in cuneiform on clay tablets and produced some of the most beautiful cylinder seals of all Mesopotamian history.

Above: A sculpture depicting a goat feeding on a bush is one of the extraordinary treasures found in the royal cemetery at Ur, Iraq. It is made of wood, sheet gold, silver, shell, and the semiprecious stone lapis lazuli, held together by bitumen (hard tar).

Below: Cylinder seals were about 1–3 inches (2–7 cm) long, but formed a rectangular imprint when rolled over a clay tablet.

Below: One of the most famous ziggurats was at Ur, built by the Sumerians in around 2100 BCE.

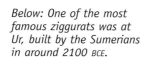

Cylinder Seals

The ancient Mesopotamians wrote letters and documents on clay tablets. To make a personal kind of signature on a tablet, in a way that could not be copied, people used cylinder seals. These were small cylinders of hard stone delicately carved with images of animals, plants, mythological figures, the gods, symbols, and so on. Rolled over the surface of the damp clay, the cylinder seals left an impression of these images. The best cylinder seals show an exceptional delicacy in carving, as well as a great skill in composition and a lively artistic imagination.

SHOWCASE: VICTORY STELE OF NARAM-SIN

One of the most celebrated pieces of Akkadian sculpture is the Victory Stele of Naram-Sin. A stele is a stone slab erected as a monument (rather like a tombstone) and decorated with relief carving or inscribed with writing. Naram-Sin (reigned c. 2254–2218 BCE) was the grandson of King Sargon I of Akkad. The stele portrays the king standing in triumph over his defeated enemies, mountain dwellers called the Lullubi.

The stele is made of pink limestone. The image was achieved by chipping away the surface stone so the picture stands out in relief from the background.

Symbols of the sun shine down on Naram-Sin, as if to confirm his godlike status.

Naram-Sin claimed he was a god-king. Wearing a horned helmet, symbol of the gods, he is portrayed much larger than any other figure. All the other figures look up to him.

Defeated enemies are being trampled under foot, or make gestures of submission.

The stele has been broken, possibly when it was taken from Sippar to the city of Susa by the Elamites in the 12th century BCE.

Left: A golden rhyton (ceremonial drinking horn), with its spout fashioned as a winged lion, was found at the site of the Persian city of Ecbatana, Iran.

Assyria

In about 1350 BCE a powerful empire arose in northern Mesopotamia. First it was based in its capital Ashur, from which the word *Assyrian* is derived. Then the capital moved to Nimrud, and then to Nineveh. These were rich, powerful, walled cities, filled with palaces and temples. Famous features of Assyrian architecture include pairs of huge winged bulls with human heads, magnificently carved from stone; they were placed on either side of doorways to create impressive entrances. By 650 BCE, the Assyrians had conquered most of the Near East and Egypt and had the largest empire the world had yet seen. Many of their numerous relief sculptures illustrate their triumphs in war and in lion hunting.

Below: A relief sculpture from the royal palace of Nineveh depicts a lioness in her death throes. Lion hunting was the sport of the Assyrian kings.

Persia

In about 547 BCE, the Persian empire arose from an area now in Iran, and quickly went on to conquer the lands formerly occupied by the Assyrians. By 490 BCE, under King Darius I (the Great; reigned 521–486 BCE), the empire stretched from the Indus Valley right across the Near East to Greece. His capital was at Susa, but he also created a ceremonial capital at Persepolis, with a palace, royal tombs, and an impressive audience hall called the Apadana. The walls were decorated with relief carvings showing subject nations bringing tribute in a ceremony that took place at Persepolis each spring. The Persian Empire, and Persepolis, were destroyed by Alexander the Great in 333–331 BCE.

Below: Persian archers are depicted in a decorative frieze made of glazed bricks, from the palace of Darius the Great at Susa, Iran.

Egyptian Architecture and Painting

The ancient Egyptian civilization lasted about 3,000 years, starting in about 3100 BCE, and ending with the death of Queen Cleopatra, and Roman occupation, in 30 BCE. This was a highly sophisticated society, ruled by the pharaohs, who were treated like living gods. The ancient Egyptians had a firm belief in their gods and the afterlife, and almost all their artistic and creative work was devoted to religious buildings and tombs. They believed that the afterlife was very much like this life, so their tombs were filled with things that the dead might need, such as furniture, food, weapons, and games, and they were decorated with images of life in Egypt. Tombs were buried to hide them from thieves, with the result that many survived almost intact until modern times, providing us with detailed images of the ancient Egyptian civilization, and rich artistic treasures.

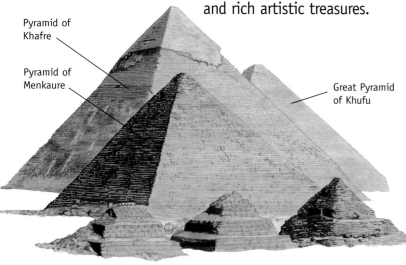

Pyramid of Khafre

Pyramid of Menkaure

Great Pyramid of Khufu

Above: Of the three main pyramids at Giza, only Khafre's has kept some of its original outer casing (seen at the top). One of the three small pyramids in the foreground may have been used for the burial of Menkaure's queen.

The Pyramids

The three pyramids of Giza, near Cairo, were built as tombs for three kings who reigned between 2585 and 2510 BCE: Khufu (also known by his Greek name, Cheops), Khafre (Chephren), and Menkaure (Mycerinus). The largest, called the Great Pyramid, was the first of the three, and was built for Khufu. All three represent outstanding feats of building and engineering.

The Great Pyramid contains over 2.3 million blocks of stone, cut with great precision and each weighing at least 2.5 tons. It was probably built during Khufu's reign, which lasted 23 years: This meant laying an average of 273 blocks every day. It is estimated that some 40,000 workers were needed. The pyramids were originally faced with smooth, polished limestone, so they shimmered in the sun.

Painted Relief

High officials in the pharaoh's court also had fine tombs. From the outside, their tombs looked like low buildings, and were called mastabas (benches). Inside, the walls were decorated with painting and relief sculpture. Both these decorative techniques were used in the mastaba of Mereruka, chief minister to King Teti (reigned c. 2350–2338 BCE). Located at the burial grounds of Saqqara, south of Giza, this was the largest private tomb of its day, with 32 rooms in all, some of which were for his wife, princess Watethathor, the daughter of Teti, and his son Meryteti.

Above: Many of the painted relief sculptures that decorate the walls of the tomb of Mereruka, in Saqqara, show beautifully drawn figures. Here, servants carry a haunch of beef and a duck.

The Great Sphinx

The pyramids at Giza are guarded by the giant statue of a mythical creature called the sphinx, with the body of a lion and a human face. It was carved from a limestone outcrop and measures 240 feet (73 m) long and 66 feet (20 m) high. The sphinx was an image of the sky god Horus. The pharaohs were associated with Horus, and sphinxes are shown wearing the striped headcloth of the pharaohs. The Great Sphinx stands in front of the pyramid of Khafre and was probably created at the same time, in about 2540 BCE.

Below: The Great Sphinx may be a portrait of Pharaoh Khafre; a much smaller stone sculpture of Khafre has very similar facial features.

SHOWCASE: FOWLING IN THE MARSHES

A picture from a tomb wall, dating to around 1350 BCE, shows a man standing on a small boat in the marshes, pursuing the gentleman's sport of hunting birds. This is Nebamun, a scribe, whose tomb was found at Thebes in southern Egypt. His wife is pictured standing behind him, and his son beneath him. The image looks as if it might show a real scene from Nebamun's life, but in fact it depicts an idealized vision of Nebamun going hunting in the afterlife.

Life in Egypt depended on the Nile River, which brought vital water to the farms on its banks. Hence the Nile had deep sacred significance.

Painters were skilled at depicting animals, including birds in flight, here watched by a cat.

The picture is full of symbolism, which an ancient Egyptian would have easily understood. For instance, the tilapia fish was considered a symbol of rebirth, or life after death.

Egyptian faces were almost always painted in profile (from the side), with the body turned toward the viewer.

Egyptian Temples

Egyptian temples were large stone buildings, with columns, courtyards, and covered shrines, lavishly decorated with sculpture. They were not just places of worship, but were considered to be the dwelling places of the gods. Only priests and the pharaohs could enter the inner shrines, where sacrifices and offerings were made to please the gods, who were represented by statues. During daily rituals, the statues were purified with burning incense, and clothed and fed as if they were humans. The only time that the public might glimpse the most sacred statues was during the annual temple festival, when they were paraded around the streets or taken for a trip on the Nile River.

Obelisk statues of Ramesses II

Pylon (monumental gateway) decorated with scenes of Ramesses' military victories

Above: The Temple of Luxor was built by Amenhotep III and Ramesses II between about 1360 and 1220 BCE. It was the focus of Opet, the annual festival of the chief god Amun.

Hall with columns with papyrus-shaped capitals

Sanctuary with shrine contained the statue of the god

Front courtyard

Pylon gateway

Above: Four colossal statues of Rameses II front his temple built at Abu Simbel in about 1260 BCE. The whole temple had to be moved in the 1960s, when the Aswan Dam was built.

Left: A cutaway showing the interior of an Egyptian temple

Right: A scribe was depicted in painted limestone for a tomb in Saqqara, dating to about 2475 BCE.

EGYPTIAN WRITING AND SCRIBES

The classic form of Egyptian writing is known as hieroglyphics, which means "sacred writing." It was devised in around 3000 BCE as a way of making religious inscriptions, and it always retained a highly respected status. Hieroglyphics began as picture writing, in which an idea was represented by a drawing, and there were some 1,000 such symbols. Later, pictures were used to imitate the sounds of words as well, which made the system more flexible and adaptable. Another form of writing, called hieratic (priestly), developed alongside hieroglyphics. This more flowing form of script was used by scribes, who were officials of high status. They wrote with reed pens on papyrus, a kind of paper made from the hammered stems of the papyrus plant. A further, simplified type of hieratic writing, called demotic (popular), developed in the last centuries of the Egyptian civilization. Hieroglyphics remained a complete mystery to later scholars until 1799, when the Rosetta Stone was found in Egypt. Its text, written in hieroglyphics, demotic, and Greek, allowed translators to decipher what the hieroglyphics meant, and to work out how the system had been constructed.

Left: An ointment vessel, dating from around 2240 BCE, bears King Pepy II's cartouche— the oval-ringed hieroglyph of his name.

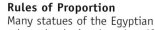

Egyptian Sculpture

The Egyptians showed exceptional talent for sculpture right from the start of their civilization. They fashioned imposing and expressive sculptures out of hard stone such as basalt, using tools made of even harder stone and abrasives such as sand. They also made strikingly realistic, painted portrait statues for tombs, which give us a vivid idea of what the Egyptians looked like 4,000 years or more after their time. One of the most extraordinary features of Egyptian art, however, is how little it changed. Many of the stylistic conventions were created in around 3000 BCE and remained virtually unaltered thereafter. Hence, through their art, the ancient Egyptians gained the reassurances of timeless continuity.

Images of the Pharaohs
The pharaohs were considered divine, providing an essential link between the gods and life on earth. They are portrayed repeatedly in sculpture as perfect human beings, with smooth, serene features and fit, healthy bodies. Such images also feature the traditional regalia worn by the pharaohs, such as the striped headcloth (*nemes*), bearing the symbol of the cobra goddess (*uraeus*), and the false beard strapped to the chin.

Left: Pepy II came to the throne at age 6 and ruled for 94 years (c. 2278–2184 BCE). Here he is depicted in alabaster, seated on his mother's knee.

Rules of Proportion
Many statues of the Egyptian pharaohs depict them in stiff, formal poses, either seated or standing. A sculpture of King Khafre (reigned c. 2555–2532 BCE), for whom the second pyramid at Giza was built, shows him with a bare torso, sitting stiffly upright, hands on knees, facing forward, gazing into eternity. He looks calm and invincible. A statue of his successor Menkaure shows him standing beside his wife with the same expression, the same upper body, and with his arms pressed to his sides, fists clenched. These images of the ideal physique were devised from carefully calculated mathematical proportions, based on a grid. The statues are almost symmetrical: In the case of the standing statues, symmetry is broken only by the left leg and foot, placed half a step in front of the right, as if the pharaoh is walking slowly, but determinedly, forward. Such stylistic sculptures, first produced in the early centuries of the ancient Egyptian civilization, set the pattern for royal portraits that was used for some 2,500 years.

Above: A basalt statue from Karnak, in southern Egypt, shows Pharaoh Thutmose III (reigned c. 1479–25 BCE) in the classical standing pose.

SHOWCASE: FUNERARY MASK OF TUTANKHAMEN

The boy-king Tutankhamen reigned for about 10 years in c. 1333–1324 BCE, and died when he was only about 18 years old. He was not a significant pharaoh—except for one thing. In 1922, his tomb was discovered. Hidden in the Valley of the Kings, it had remained almost intact, undiscovered by grave robbers, for over 3,000 years. It contained scores of exquisite artifacts: sculpture, jewelry, carved furniture, board games, weapons, chariots, pottery, and basketwork. Among the greatest of the treasures was the funerary mask of Tutankhamen, a life-size portrait in solid gold.

Below: The mummified body of Tutankhamen was placed in a set of three coffins, one inside the other. Each was in the shape of the king, arms folded and holding the royal symbols of the crook and the flail.

The two outer coffins were made of gilded wood, glass, and semi-precious stones.

The gold funerary mask was placed over the mummy.

The innermost coffin was made of solid gold, weighing 2,447 pounds (1,110 kg).

These symbols represented rule over all Egypt—the cobra for Lower Egypt, and the vulture's head for Upper Egypt.

The stripes of the nemes headcloth are made of blue glass.

The face has the same expression used to portray pharaohs throughout Egyptian history.

The collar is inlaid with semiprecious stones.

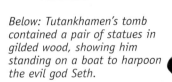

Below: Tutankhamen's tomb contained a pair of statues in gilded wood, showing him standing on a boat to harpoon the evil god Seth.

Right: The painted limestone bust of Queen Nefertiti, wife of Akhenaten, comes from a brief period of more naturalistic royal sculpture.

Convention Versus Creativity
There was a formal, official side to Egyptian sculpture, produced for the temples and for the glorification of the pharaohs and gods. While impressive, it can also be repetitive, with limited human expression. This was deliberate: Royalty had to be portrayed with strict, formal conventions, in keeping with their divinity. But artists could treat lesser beings more freely, both in painting and sculpture. In particular, Egyptian

sculptors showed their imagination and flair in painted portrait sculpture, where they produced more relaxed, spontaneous poses, full of character and humanity. The only time this rule was broken was during the reign of Pharaoh Akhenaten (c.1353–1336 BCE), who led a short-lived religious revolution from his new capital of Amarna. During this time, royalty were also depicted in a more relaxed way. But it was the exception that proved the rule: Shortly after his reign, artists returned once again to the formal conventions.

Right: Sculptors were particularly inventive in the portrayal of sacred animals. This glazed pottery hippopotamus also shows the water and river plants in which it wallows.

Art of the Aegean

While the ancient Egyptians flourished in North Africa, new and very different Bronze Age civilizations were emerging across the Mediterranean Sea to the north, based on seafaring and trading. They appeared first in about 3000 BCE in the Cyclades, a set of some 30 islands in the southern Aegean Sea. Then the focus moved south to the larger island of Crete, which was dominated by the Minoan civilization from about 2000 BCE. In around 1450 BCE, the warlike city-states of the Mycenaeans, on mainland Greece, took control of the region. Each in its own distinctive way laid the foundations for the Greek civilization that was to follow.

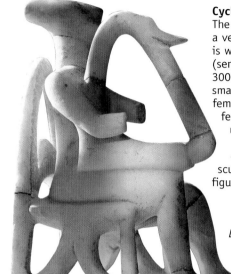

Cycladic Sculpture
The islands of the Cyclades produce a very beautiful kind of marble that is white and sometimes translucent (semi-transparent). From around 3000 BCE this was sculpted into small figurines, typically naked female forms that may have been fertility symbols. The heads usually have flat faces with a nose, and little or no indication of the mouth or eyes. Later sculptures depicted seated male figures playing harps or pipes.

Left: Just 8 inches (21 cm) high, this Cycladic harp player was sculpted from marble in about 2200 BCE.

Minoan Pottery
The Minoans showed a real verve for design with their pottery. The Kamares style, named after a sacred cave in Crete, dates to about 1900–1700 BCE. Pitchers, dishes, and bowls were decorated in dark colors with swirling geometric patterns and stylized shells and plants. After about 1700, potters decorated their work with bold images of plants and animals (such as bulls, octopuses, and dolphins), all invigorated with the same feel for design.

Above: A beaked pitcher from the Minoan city of Phaistos has been painted with the exuberant patterns typical of the Kamares style.

THE PALACE AT KNOSSOS

The remains of a huge ancient palace were excavated at Knossos, in northern Crete, over some 30 years after 1900. It was said to be the palace of the legendary King Minos, after whom the Minoan civilization was named. It seems that the palace was occupied in two phases. The first phase lasted from about 1900 to 1700 BCE. Then this palace, along with others in Crete, was destroyed, perhaps by an earthquake. A new palace was later built on the same site, and lasted to about 1400 BCE. Many of the rooms were decorated with wall paintings featuring people, animals, and plants stylishly designed, vividly colored, and full of a joyous enthusiasm for life and nature.

It appears that the Minoans were a prosperous people who took pleasure in life's comforts and luxuries. The large storerooms beneath the palace were filled with grain, olive oil, wine, and other goods. These may have given rise to the Greek legend that related how, beneath the palace, there was a labyrinth where King Minos kept the monstrous Minotaur, which had the body of a man and the head of a bull. The Minoans show little sign of being warlike: This may be why the more aggressive Mycenaeans took control of Crete and the other Minoan islands in about 1450 BCE.

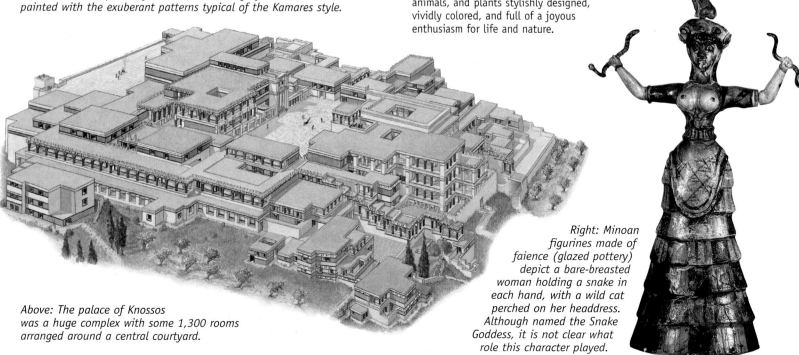

Above: The palace of Knossos was a huge complex with some 1,300 rooms arranged around a central courtyard.

Right: Minoan figurines made of faience (glazed pottery) depict a bare-breasted woman holding a snake in each hand, with a wild cat perched on her headdress. Although named the Snake Goddess, it is not clear what role this character played.

Mycenaean Art

The Mycenaeans are named after the ancient city of Mycenae, but there were a number of other similar cities on the Greek mainland, such as Athens, Tiryns, Pylos, and Thebes. Their warlike nature is reflected in the massive stone fortifications that they built to protect their palaces. Their art is similar to that of the Minoans, but is rather stiffer and more formal, and tends to focus on more aggressive themes, such as warriors and hunting. The Mycenaeans' big rivals were the Trojans from the city of Troy on the Asian side of the Aegean Sea. According to legend, and Homer's epic poem the *Iliad*, this gave rise to the 10-year siege of Troy, led by Agamemnon, King of Mycenae. This legend seems to relate to a real war that took place in about 1250 BCE.

Above: A Mycenaean pottery vase is decorated with a line of marching warriors, drawn with the kind of bold outline used by the Minoans.

Left: The Mycenaeans buried treasures with their dead royalty, such as this golden funerary mask. It is known as the Mask of Agamemnon but probably belongs to an earlier era, around 1500 BCE.

Right: The Lion Gate, built into the thick city walls of Mycenae, includes delicate carvings of two lions— perhaps the oldest example of public sculpture in Greece.

SHOWCASE: THE BULL-LEAPING FRESCO AT THE PALACE AT KNOSSOS

A famous wall painting, dating to around 1500 BCE, appears to depict the sport of bull-leaping. Bulls were considered to be sacred animals throughout the region, and this dangerous sport was perhaps connected to a religious ritual. Athletes would grab the bull's horns, somersault onto its back, and then somersault again to land behind the bull. The painting has all the lively charm and vigor that is typical of Minoan art.

The fresco has been heavily restored. Enough of the original painting (the darker colors) survived to work out what it might have looked like.

This picture may perhaps illustrate an athlete going through the process of bull-leaping, showing him in three positions between takeoff and landing, like a cartoon strip.

Fresco is a way of making durable wall paintings. Colors are painted onto patches of fresh (Italian: *fresco*) plaster before it dries.

A distinctive feature of Minoan art is the use of flat areas of color without shading.

THE ORDERS OF COLUMNS

The ancient Greeks developed three main styles of architecture, which are most easily recognizable from the style of the carved columns and their capitals (the decorative tops of the columns). The simplest, oldest, and heaviest style was the Doric order, named after the Dorians but developed in the 7th century BCE: The columns were fluted (carved with vertical grooves), with a simple square capital at the top. Next came the Ionic order, named after Ionia, a region of ancient Greece in western Asia, where the style developed in the 6th century BCE; it had more slender, fluted columns, and scroll-shaped capitals. Then there was the Corinthian order, named after the city of Corinth, and said to have been invented by an architect called Callimachus in the 5th century BCE; its slender, fluted columns were topped by elaborate capitals featuring scrolls and acanthus leaves. Each of these orders also had accompanying styles of entablature—the set of bands and friezes and the triangular pediment that lay between the top of the capital and the roofline when viewed from the front of the building (typically a temple).

Left: The Doric column and capital were the simplest among the three orders.

Right: The Ionic column is easy to recognize from its scroll-shaped capital.

Right: A capital of sculpted acanthus leaves set the Corinthian column apart.

Greek Architecture

Above: The Porch of the Caryatids is one of the most striking features of the Erechtheum, on the Acropolis of Athens. A caryatid is a column sculpted in the form of a female figure.

The Mycenaean civilization collapsed in around 1125 BCE, perhaps as a result of invasions by the Dorians, warriors from the north armed with weapons made of a new, stronger, and sharper metal: iron. Four hundred years of Dark Ages followed, before a set of vibrant city-states emerged in around 700 BCE. They included Athens, Corinth, Sparta, and Thebes. They entered into ever-changing alliances with one another, but together formed what we call ancient Greece. These cities rapidly developed a new, stately, and sophisticated style of architecture, decorated with some of the greatest stone sculpture ever made. Athens grew in power and prosperity, especially after defeating the Persians in 480 BCE, and it enjoyed a Golden Age until 431 BCE.

Right: A cutaway illustration shows how a Greek temple was designed.

The most important cult statue stood in the main, windowless interior room, called the cella.

The surrounding outer rows of columns formed the peristyle.

Behind the cella was the treasury, a storehouse of precious cult objects and offerings.

The whole temple stood on a raised stone platform or stylobate, reached by steps.

The Acropolis of Athens

Many Greek cities had an acropolis (high city), a protected area built on the highest piece of land, which could be defended against attackers. An acropolis was often where the city had begun, so it took on a sacred significance. The most famous is the Acropolis of Athens, set on a rocky, flat-topped escarpment that rises sharply above the surrounding city. Inhabited since Neolithic times, it became the site of Athens's most precious temples, dedicated primarily to the city's protective goddess, Athena. It was here that the Parthenon was built in 447–432 BCE, at a time when the whole site underwent complete redevelopment. The other major buildings on the Acropolis, built at the same time, are the Propylaea (the monumental gateway of columns), the Erechtheum (a temple complex), and the temple of Athena Nike (Athena the Victorious).

The Greek Temple

Greek temples were constructed as earthly homes for the gods, which were represented by a sacred statue. Most were built to a standard format: rectangular, with columns lining the sides supporting a gable roof set at a shallow angle. The entrance was on one of the shorter sides. The ancient Greeks did not use arches to support their buildings; instead, they used columns and horizontal beams. Temples also had open-air altars, for animal sacrifices.

SHOWCASE: THE PARTHENON

By applying mathematics and ideal proportions, the architects of ancient Greece achieved a sense of harmony and grace that has rarely been matched since. There is no greater example of this than the Parthenon. It was built in white marble on the Acropolis of Athens in 447–432 BCE to the designs of Kallikrates and Iktinos, under the direction of the sculptor Pheidias (c. 490–430 BCE). Inside was a huge statue of Athena Parthenos (Athena the Virgin) by Phidias, made of gold, ivory, and marble.

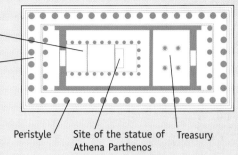

Cella

Portico

Peristyle   Site of the statue of   Treasury
             Athena Parthenos

Below and below right: The Parthenon was built in Doric style, as seen in the form of the columns and capitals. The exterior was originally richly decorated with painted marble statues and friezes of relief statues.

Above right: The ground plan of the Parthenon shows its highly ordered, symmetrical construction. This is an octastyle design, meaning that the front is lined with eight columns. The portico (entrance porch) contains two ranks of columns.

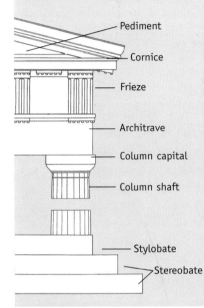

Pediment

Cornice

Frieze

Architrave

Column capital

Column shaft

Stylobate

Stereobate

The Greek Theater

The ancient Greeks founded the basis of modern Western theater. Their traditions began in about 550 BCE with religious festivals held in honor of the god Dionysus: Song-and-dance entertainment formed part of the rituals. This developed into plays. Later, writers created comedies and tragedies, usually performed by a few main characters (played by masked male actors) backed by a chanting chorus. Such performances were hugely popular, and vast outdoor theaters were built to seat large audiences. Semicircular ranks of stone seats were built into a scooped-out hillside around the acting area and stage. The acoustics were remarkable: Low voices and whispers onstage could be heard even in the outermost seats.

Left: The theater at Epidaurus was built in about 350 BCE and could seat 18,000 spectators. In the warm, dry weather of Greece, outdoor theaters were a practical way of hosting large-scale entertainment.

Hellenistic Architecture

In 336 BCE Alexander the Great (reigned 336–323 BCE) began his extraordinary conquests. Shortly after becoming king of Macedonia (a neighbor of Greece) at the age of 20, he led his armies into Asia, and by the time of his death at the age of just 33, he ruled an empire stretching from Greece to northern India, and including Egypt, Persia, and Mesopotamia. His new empire spread the ideas of Greek culture, particularly in Asia Minor (modern Turkey). Called Hellenistic (after *Hellenes*, the Greeks' name for themselves), its art and architecture was highly refined, but also grandiose and monumental, a reflection of the power and wealth of the cities—such as Pergamum, Antioch, and Alexandria—that developed in the wake of Alexander's conquests. Temples, tombs, and public buildings were built in this grand Greek style, richly decorated with dramatic sculpture.

Below: The Altar of Zeus, from Pergamum, built in 165–156 BCE, is a massive structure decorated with a sculpted frieze 371 feet (118 m) long depicting a great struggle between the gods and giants. It was taken to Berlin, Germany, and reconstructed in the 19th century.

Right: By the time this statue was carved in around 500 BCE, sculpture had become more realistic. Functioning like a kouros as a grave-marker, this was a funerary portrait for a man called Aristodikos.

Left: This superb Greek statue of a warrior was cast in bronze in about 430 BCE. Lost in a shipwreck off Riace, Italy, in ancient times, it was rediscovered in 1972.

Evolution of Greek Statues

The earliest Greek statues depicting the human form, from the so-called Archaic period (c. 800–500 BCE), featured nude male figures called kouroi (singular: kouros, meaning "male youth"). Standing stiffly upright, arms to their sides, left foot half a pace forward, they bear many similarities to Egyptian sculptures of the pharaohs (see page 12). Typically, the kouroi are beardless and have long hair in ringlets; their eyes are closed, and they have a half-smile on their lips. Some are life-size, while others three or four times larger; they were often made for temples, as votive offerings to please the gods, or to mark graves, although they were never intended as portraits. Over time, figures became less stylized, and more relaxed and naturalistic, with the arms making freer gestures, and the head slightly turned. But nonetheless, certain features remain consistent. These are idealized images of the male physique, with the torsos in particular indicating fitness and muscular strength.

Left: Kouroi did not usually depict individuals, but an inscription states that this kouros, which dates to about 580 BCE, depicts Biton, a hero from Greek legend.

Greek Sculpture

Ancient Greek sculpture made after about 500 BCE set the standard for Western sculpture for 2,500 years. One of the tasks that Greek sculptors gave themselves was to create highly lifelike, naturalistic, three-dimensional replicas of human beings. They were also concerned with portraying human ideals of physical beauty, strength, and courage, in ever more ambitious compositions. They achieved this even when hewing their work out of hard stone, such as marble, but they also used bronze cast from clay models. The sculptures we see today are often not what the artists had intended: Greek stone sculpture was painted in vivid colors, and all sculpture might include elements made of wood, metal, and ivory that have since been lost.

Kouroi and Kore

The female equivalent of the kouroi were statues depicting clothed young women called korai (singular: kore, "maiden"). Made in the Archaic period, between about 600 and 500 BCE, they served the same function as kouroi at temples and grave sites. Their gently smiling faces look serene, and their graceful aspect is underlined by the careful depiction of the long, soft drapery that covers their bodies. The pose is essentially the same as that of the kouroi, except one hand may be raised, or lifting the dress to keep it out of the way of the advancing foot.

Above: A kore from the island of Chios, dating from about 510 BCE, still bears the traces of color that once made her into a fully painted, lifelike statue.

THE LOST-WAX PROCESS

The Greeks made bronze statues by using the lost-wax process. It meant that a number of copies could be made of a single original. First, the artist made a sculpture in clay (1). A plaster cast was then made of this sculpture (2); when cut away, a precise impression of the original sculpture remained on the inside of the mold. Then molten beeswax was poured into the mold (3). Then the mold was carefully removed, leaving a wax copy of the original sculpture. The wax model was filled with earth and a metal skeleton for support (4). Wax sprues (branchlike rods) were then attached to the wax model to provide channels though which the molten bronze would flow (5). Another mold was made by encasing the wax model and sprues in a shell of wet clay. The wax was then removed ("lost") by heating the shell (6), then molten bronze was poured in to replace it (7). When the shell was broken away, the bronze sculpture was revealed (8). The sculpture was then chased with metal tools to tidy it up. Large bronze statues were made in several pieces, which were then welded together.

Right: The stages of the lost-wax process.

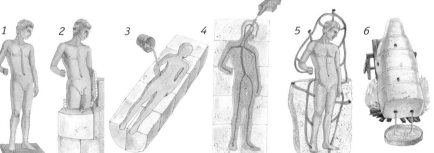

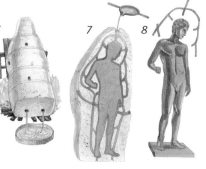

SHOWCASE: PHEIDIAS, THE FRIEZE RELIEFS OF THE PARTHENON

There is a crosscurrent of movement: The horses move forward, while a rider turns back, and the standing man, dressed in a togalike himation, signals to the rear.

The horses rear up, as if impatient at the progress of the procession, underlining a feeling of suppressed energy.

Above: Although missing its head and arms, the sculpture of Nike (goddess of victory), found on the island of Samothrace, is celebrated for its sense of movement. It dates to about 200 BCE.

The riders form part of a lively and somewhat chaotic procession of horsemen following chariots.

The images are sculpted in low relief; originally they would have been painted in bright colors.

The frieze consisted of 115 separate plaques, which fit together to form continuous images along the north, east, west, and south sides of the cella. This plaque comes from the north side.

Pheidias was one of the greatest sculptors of ancient Greece. He created the giant statue of Zeus at Olympia (since destroyed), one of the Seven Wonders of the Ancient World. He also oversaw the building of the Parthenon and was responsible for much of the sculpture. This included the frieze that decorated the outer, upper part of the cella, which depicts a procession during the Great Panathenaea, a festival held every four years in honor of the goddess Athena. Some 524 feet (160 m) long and 3 feet (1 m) high, it contains 360 humans figures and 250 animals, capturing their movement and excitement with astonishing verve.

Hellenistic Sculpture

By the 4th century BCE, Greek sculpture had acquired even greater confidence. More emphasis was given to creating compositions in the round, to be seen from all angles. The figures became even more relaxed, supple, and naturalistic, and sculptors became more daring, turning blocks of marble into ambitious compositions with several figures, in complex poses and with projecting limbs. The female nude, usually portraying goddesses, became a popular subject, while the treatment of clothing was especially effective, often creating the illusion of virtually transparent cloth covering a living body beneath. Faces, and particularly portraits, conveyed a real sense of character and individuality. By the 1st century BCE, Greek sculpture had achieved an astonishing complexity, much admired and imitated by the Romans.

Left: The bronze head of a god or hero, with its finely rendered hair, evokes a strong sense of character.

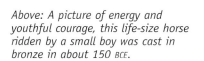

Above: A picture of energy and youthful courage, this life-size horse ridden by a small boy was cast in bronze in about 150 BCE.

Greek Ceramics

Painting was an important art form in ancient Greece. Artists produced large wall paintings, but very few of these have survived, and what little we know of them comes mainly from descriptions in ancient texts. However, we have a clear indication of the high standards of Greek painting from another source: pottery. A very large number of Greek pottery vases, dishes, jugs, and other vessels have come down to us, and they show exceptional talent for drawing, painting, and design. While in most ancient civilizations vase painting was not considered high art, in ancient Greece it became a highly developed medium, ranking alongside sculpture and wall painting, and attracting artists of the highest caliber. Many vase painters signed their work, and so are known by name.

Above: A wine pitcher (jug) from the Orientalizing period (7th century BCE) shows repeated images of deer and swans, set out in an almost geometric pattern.

Bands of intricate geometric patterns run all around the vase.

THE EVOLUTION OF VASE PAINTING IN ANCIENT GREECE

The Minoans had shown a distinctive approach to pottery decoration, combining bold, imaginative painting with a highly developed sense of design (see page 14). The Mycenaeans borrowed from the Minoan style, but this tradition was lost in the Dark Ages that followed the collapse of the Mycenaean civilization in about 1125 BCE. For several centuries, potters of the Greek mainland produced only simple ware, decorated with bands of color, wavy lines, and simple patterns. This Proto-Geometric period was followed in the 10th century BCE by the Geometric period, when artists began decorating vases with bolder abstract patterns and shapes. During the 8th century BCE, human figures began to appear in pottery decoration, at first as simple stylized forms that were treated as

part of the geometric design. By this time, potters had perfected the forms of the vessels themselves, which were produced in various standard shapes to a very high quality of finish. Figures—of human beings and animals—gradually came to predominate in the subsequent Orientalizing period, so called because the Greeks came into contact with Eastern civilizations and absorbed motifs more familiar to us from Egyptian or Mesopotamian art. This style led, in about 700 BCE, to the development of the so-called black-figure technique, where black figures are shown in silhouette against the light red natural color of the clay. In around 530 BCE, a new red-figure painting technique was invented, which reversed the earlier color scheme, with red figures depicted on black backgrounds.

This central band depicts mourners surrounding a dead body, which is lying on a funeral bed beneath a canopy.

Right: An Athenian vase painter at work on a vase in his workshop. The vase has been placed on a turntable, which helped to create an even, all-around design.

Above: This elaborately decorated vase is a perfect example of the late Geometric period, dating to about 740 BCE. Standing some 5 feet (1.5 m) tall, it was placed over a warrior's tomb in the Dipylon cemetery of Athens, as a grave marker.

Right: Simple freehand spirals, neatly arranged, decorate this vase of the Proto-Geometric period.

SHOWCASE: THE FRANÇOIS VASE

The François Vase dates from the early 7th century BCE and is one of the finest examples of early black-figure work. Of very high quality, it is also important because it is one of the earliest vases that is signed both by the potter ("Ergotimos made it") and the painter ("Kleitas drew it"). This suggests that vase painting was a prestigious profession with well-known artists.

The vase is a krater, a large vessel with a broad rim that was used to mix wine with water before serving.

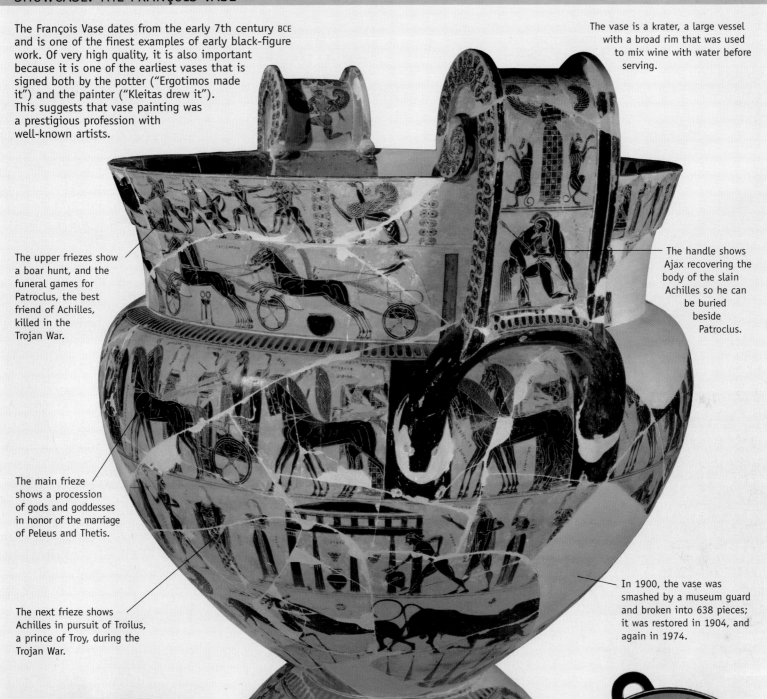

The upper friezes show a boar hunt, and the funeral games for Patroclus, the best friend of Achilles, killed in the Trojan War.

The handle shows Ajax recovering the body of the slain Achilles so he can be buried beside Patroclus.

The main frieze shows a procession of gods and goddesses in honor of the marriage of Peleus and Thetis.

The next frieze shows Achilles in pursuit of Troilus, a prince of Troy, during the Trojan War.

In 1900, the vase was smashed by a museum guard and broken into 638 pieces; it was restored in 1904, and again in 1974.

Above: A krater (wine vase) depicting Hercules wrestling is typical of the exceptional red-figure work by the vase painter Euphronios, who was active from about 520–470 BCE.

Black- and Red-Figure Vases

The black-figure style involved not just painting black figures onto the red clay, but also painting fine details in white or red, or incising them with a sharp object (thus cutting through the paint to reveal the red background). By contrast, with the red-figure vases, the backgrounds were painted black, around the figures of bare red clay (a more realistic color). The vases were fired in kilns in three stages. Both black- and red-figure vases depicted scenes from Greek mythology, or scenes from daily life. The images are astonishingly precise and detailed, and vases by good artists were highly prized. As early as 600 BCE, the Greeks were exporting painted vases abroad, notably to the Etruscans in northern Italy.

Above: Exekias (active c. 550–525 BCE) produced this black-figure kylix (wine cup with handles), with a picture on its interior surface of the god Dionysus, the god of wine, in a boat.

THE ETRUSCANS

The history of Rome begins with the Etruscans, who developed a sophisticated civilization in north-western Italy, centering on Tuscany, from about 1500 BCE. Like the ancient Egyptians, the Etruscans had a firm belief that the afterlife was similar to this life, so they built large, houselike tombs for their dead, which they decorated with paintings and filled with goods. Unearthed tombs show that they were skilled potters, metalworkers, and artists. After about 700 BCE, their art became heavily influenced by the Greeks, but nevertheless it always retained a joyous character that is distinctively Etruscan and contrasts with the more serious tone of later Roman art. According to tradition, Rome was founded in 753 BCE, and the first kings of Rome were Etruscans. They were ousted in 509 BCE, but the Etruscans did not come fully under the control of Rome until 86 BCE.

Left: The Etruscan statue called the Chimera of Arezzo, dating to the 4th century BCE, shows great skill in both sculpting and bronze casting. The Chimera was a mythical hybrid monster: Here it has a lion's body, a snake for a tail, and a goat's head protruding from its back.

Roman Sculpture

Below: A Roman portrait of a woman shows the elaborate hairstyle of the Flavian dynasty of Roman emperors (69–96 CE). As with Greek sculpture, this bust would have been painted.

By 150 BCE, there was a new force in the Western world: the Romans. From their original base in Rome, they first conquered all of Italy, and then they spread across the Mediterranean, taking Hellenistic Asia Minor (modern Turkey) and then Greece itself in 146 BCE. The Romans were great admirers of Greek culture, and particularly of Greek sculpture. They had known it for centuries through trade and because there had been Greek colonies in southern Italy and Sicily since the 8th century BCE. When the Romans wanted sculpture to decorate their public buildings and their villas, they essentially wanted Greek sculpture. Greek sculptors were happy to supply the demand. Many of them went to live in Rome. They even brought their blocks of marble with them, although after 50 BCE new marble quarries were opened at Carrara, in western Italy. The one distinctive contribution that the Romans made in this field was in portrait sculpture, with their fondness for powerful, sometimes unflattering likenesses.

Above: A Roman sculpture of the 1st century BCE shows a patrician, dressed in a full toga, holding busts of his ancestors—sculptures within a sculpture.

The Republic

After the Romans had rid themselves of their Etruscan kings in 509 BCE, the state was ruled as a republic (i.e., without a hereditary monarch). There were two classes of Romans: the ordinary people (called plebeians), and the nobles (the patricians). In the early centuries of the republic, any displays of wealth or power were frowned upon, and so little sculpture was commissioned. But after about 200 BCE, habits changed. Rich and powerful patricians began to build large villas, which they decorated with sculptures—portraits of themselves and their ancestors, as well as impressive and inspiring images of athletes, philosophers, famous generals, gods, and goddesses. Sculpture became a major business. In some cases, to save time, headless bodies with ideal Greek features were mass-produced, so that individually carved portrait heads could be added to them.

Roman Copies of Greek Sculpture

Hundreds of original Greek statues were shipped from Greece to Rome, pillaged after conquest, or purchased by collectors. Copies were made of the best of them. With bronze statues, copies could be produced from molds, but marble statues had to be individually carved. The famous Medici Venus, a statue of the naked goddess now in Florence, is one of

numerous copies of an original Greek sculpture, perhaps by Praxiteles (one of the greatest sculptors of the 4th century BCE). This huge demand for sculpture provided work for studios in Greece, and for Greek sculptors working in Italy, and many of the copies were produced to a very high standard. As it happens, in many cases the original Greek sculpture has now been lost—so we know the original only through Roman copies.

Left: The Dying Gaul is a marble Roman copy of a lost Hellenistic statue. The original may have been a bronze statue by Epigonos of Pergamum, dating to about 220 BCE.

SHOWCASE: THE LUDOVISI SARCOPHAGUS

The perspective has been flattened, so the foreground and the background appear in virtually the same plane. This draws the viewer into the thick of the battle.

The Goths are long-haired, bearded, and wear trousers, all symbols of an uncouth, barbarian race in the Roman view.

Herennius Etruscus, bareheaded and on horseback, makes a triumphant gesture, but seems almost disconnected from the scene of battle, as if aware of his imminent death.

The Goths appear mainly in the lower part of the scene, being brutally crushed or captured by the Romans.

This highly elaborate sarcophagus (stone coffin) depicts a battle scene between the Romans and Goths. It honors the memory of Herennius Etruscus and his father, Emperor Decius, both of whom died in the Battle of Abrittus (in modern Bulgaria) in 251 CE. This may have been their tomb. Carved from a single huge block of marble, all four sides of the sarcophagus are covered with similar scenes. These are carved in deep relief in the Hellenistic manner, but the crowding of the figures—so intense that the background is almost totally obscured—is unusual. When first made, the stone would have been painted.

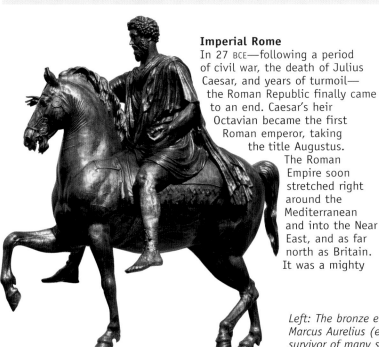

Imperial Rome

In 27 BCE—following a period of civil war, the death of Julius Caesar, and years of turmoil—the Roman Republic finally came to an end. Caesar's heir Octavian became the first Roman emperor, taking the title Augustus.

The Roman Empire soon stretched right around the Mediterranean and into the Near East, and as far north as Britain. It was a mighty military power, controlled from Rome for over three centuries by a series of ruling dynasties. Some emperors were exceptionally talented, others criminally incompetent, but they all shared the desire to present a public image of glory, might, and dignity to inspire their subjects and underline their right to rule. Sculpture played a key role in this public relations exercise, with portraits and large statues, and triumphal arches and columns illustrating the emperors' victories. The grandiose sculpture of Hellenistic Greece provided a good model.

Left: The bronze equestrian (horse-riding) statue of Marcus Aurelius (emperor 161–180 CE) is a rare survivor of many such statues of the emperors.

Above: This marble head of Constantine (emperor 306–337 CE) came from a colossal seated statue that was placed—like a statue of a god in a Greek temple—in his basilica, a public building in the Forum of Rome.

Below: Rising to four stories, the Porta Nigra (Black Gate) at Trier, in Germany, was built in about 200 CE and formed part of the city walls.

Roman Temples

Roman temples followed the patterns set by the Greeks and the Etruscans. The main focus was an enclosed chamber, or cella, containing a statue of the god or goddess to whom the temple was dedicated. This was surrounded by columns in the Greek manner, but Roman temples did not generally have a peristyle, with rows of freestanding columns all around the building. Instead, the sides and back of the cella came close to the edge of the platform and were decorated with half-columns. Most ceremonies and sacrifices—of oxen, sheep, goats, pigs, chickens, doves—took place at altars in front of the temple.

Above: The Greek influence is evident in the Maison Carrée at Nîmes, France, a temple built in about 19 BCE.

Roman Cities

The Romans controlled their empire from towns and cities linked by a network of well-surfaced, straight roads. Many cities began as fortified military camps but soon developed the kind of sophisticated infrastructure for which the Romans have become famous: with paved streets, running water, drainage, under-floor heating systems, and public baths. At the center was the forum, an open space that served as a market, but also was the center of trade and finance, decision making, and government. The forum was often the site of the most important temples. Many cities also had theaters and amphitheaters, where gladiators fought.

Roman Architecture

In architecture, the Romans looked to the Greeks for models of perfect proportion, style, and grace. They adopted the three orders of Greek architecture for their columns (see page 16), favoring particularly the Corinthian style. But there was one major difference in their architecture: The Romans used the arch (although they did not invent it). This gave them distinct advantages not only in style, but also in strength. By using the arch, the Romans could build pierced structures to a far greater height than the Greeks. This is seen notably in their bridges and gateways, and aqueducts such as the Pont du Gard in France, one of the many engineering triumphs that underpinned the Roman Empire. The Romans used a semicircular arch, which—taken one step further—allowed them also to build domes.

Above and left: The indents, or coffers, in the dome of the Pantheon were created by pouring concrete into moulds. The result is not just a strong structure, but also a pleasing effect.

The Pantheon

In about 27 BCE, Marcus Vipsanius Agrippa, a close adviser to Augustus, built a temple to all the gods, bearing the Greek name the Pantheon (*pan* = all, *theos* = god). After a fire, it was rebuilt under Emperor Hadrian in 120–124 CE. Although converted into a church in 609, it has remained virtually intact. This was the largest dome of the ancient world, measuring 141 feet (43 m) in both height and diameter. Its great size was made possible by the invention of concrete. No other concrete structure of this scale was attempted until the 20th century.

The front of the Pantheon resembled a Greek temple.

Statues of the gods were placed in niches around the inner walls.

An opening, or oculus, in the center of the dome lets in the light, and also the rain.

Above: The Arch of Constantine in Rome was built in 315 CE to celebrate Emperor Constantine's battle that left him as sole ruler, after a period of turmoil and divided rule.

The Empire

Although the Romans were militaristic and almost constantly at war, much of the empire enjoyed long stretches of peace, notably during the period of the early empire known as Pax Romana (Roman Peace), from 27 BCE to 180 CE. During stable times, the Romans were able to bring the considerable benefits of their rule to the people of their empire, such as their skills in engineering and building. The combination of Greek-style columns and proportions coupled with arches became the Roman style, and this spread throughout the Roman Empire.

Right: Petra, the secretive trading city of the Nabataeans in Jordan, was ruled by the Romans after 106 CE. Its buildings, carved out of rock, show the influence of Roman style.

SHOWCASE: THE COLOSSEUM

The Colosseum in Rome was begun by Emperor Vespasian; it took 10 years to build and was completed in 80 CE during the reign of Emperor Titus. For over 400 years it was the setting for spectacular games, including gladiatorial fights, contests between men and wild animals, and races. At first it was known as the Great Flavian Amphitheater; Vespasian and Titus belonged to the Flavian dynasty. *Amphi* means "two" in Greek: This was like two Greek semicircular theaters (see page 17) joined together to make a complete circle. The popular name Colosseum was probably a reference to a huge statue of Emperor Nero, also called the Colosseum, that once stood nearby. But the Colosseum itself is indeed colossal: It stands 187 feet (57 m) high and has a circumference of 1,729 feet (527 m).

The exterior is decorated by columns in the three Greek orders: Doric, Ionic, and Corinthian.

There were statues of the gods in the arches of the two upper floors.

There were enough seats for 50,000 people.

Stone brackets, seen on the outside, supported timber masts and a huge sheet of cloth that was used to shade spectators from the sun.

The arrangement of stairs and passages inside was ingeniously designed to cope with large numbers of spectators; it has served as a model for stadiums ever since.

Passages led under the stage to elevator shafts, through which gladiators and animals could be raised into the arena.

Wall Decoration

If the villas of Pompeii are anything to go by, the houses and villas of well-to-do Romans were richly decorated with paintings. These paintings were frescoes: The pigment was applied to damp plaster; when the plaster was dry, it could be finished with tempera (pigment mixed with egg yolk as a binder). Popular subjects included rural and agricultural landscapes, still lifes of fruit or fish, and mythological scenes with figures and animals. The illusion of depth was achieved by trompe l'oeil effects (effects that deliberately trick the eye), with receding architecture, fake sculpture, and receding landscapes—all of which reveal a good grasp of perspective.

Left: The Villa of the Mysteries in Pompeii is named after the frescoes that appear to depict some kind of ceremony.

Roman Paintings and Mosaics

Below: A still life featuring a glass vessel and green peaches shows delicate powers of observation. It comes from a wall painting in Herculaneum.

As in sculpture and architecture, the Romans looked to Greece for guidance in painting, although they clearly also had Etruscan traditions to draw on. Most Roman painting was done on walls, and much of it by Greek craftsmen. However, very few of these wall paintings have survived—except at Pompeii and Herculaneum, two towns buried by the eruption of Mount Vesuvius in 79 CE. By contrast, mosaics are a distinctively Roman art form—and far more of these have survived.

The most elaborate mosaics depict ambitious images of battles, mythological scenes, landscapes, and still lifes, demonstrating the lively artistic imaginations of their creators.

Above: Many of the Fayum portraits depict children or young adults, an indication that most people did not live long at that time. This picture of a boy dates from the 2nd century CE.

Portraiture

Roman artists were clearly skilled at portraiture. In Roman Egypt, portrait paintings on wooden panels were placed over the faces of mummies, following the ancient tradition of funerary masks (see page 13). Many of these funerary portraits have survived in the dry climate of the Fayum district, in western Egypt. They tend to be idealized, flattering images, always looking at the viewer, but none-theless they provide a powerful impression of living members of the Roman Empire.

Styles of Roman Painting

Based largely on the paintings of Pompeii and Herculaneum, the history of Roman wall painting is usually divided into four successive styles. The first style (2nd to early 1st century BCE), known as incrustation, is distinguished by painted imitations of colored marble or wood veneers, linked to architecture. The second style (1st century BCE), known as the architectural style, was largely concerned with the depiction of architectural structures and perspective, with landscapes and scenes with figures and animals seen through windowlike openings. The third style (late 1st century BCE to mid-1st century CE), known as the ornamental style, features painted frames around pictures that are presented like a gallery. The fourth style (c. 30–79 CE) involves a mixture of previous styles, including framing and trompe l'oeil (French for "trick the eye") architectural features, plus bizarre and original decorative elements known as grotesques (fanciful symmetrical decorative designs with garlands, symbols, and strange creatures).

SHOWCASE: MOSAIC FROM THE HOUSE OF THE TRAGIC POET

The House of the Tragic Poet in Pompeii gets its name from its paintings depicting scenes from Homer's *Iliad*, and the theatrical mosaic on the floor of a reception room, dating to the 1st century CE. This depicts theater actors getting ready to perform a play involving satyrs (woodland gods, half goat, half man), as can be seen from the goatskin costumes. A musician in the center tries out a double flute, while an actor gets dressed in the background.

A decorative frieze borders the top of the mosaic, featuring urns, columns, and sculptural pillars (or termini) featuring satyrs.

Roman actors always wore masks onstage, which made their characters easier to identify.

The artist shows a good understanding of spatial perspective: The people in the background clearly appear to be standing at a distance behind those in the foreground.

Darker mosaic tiles have been skillfully used to show shading, as seen in the folds of the drapery.

Step 1: The tiles are laid onto the design.

Step 2: A layer of mortar is applied to the back of the mosaic, to attach the backing cloth.

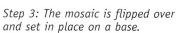

Step 3: The mosaic is flipped over and set in place on a base.

THE MOSAIC TECHNIQUE

Roman mosaics consist of hundreds of small, cubic tiles of hard, colored stone, called tesserae, which were fixed into position by mortar. They were made by specialist craftsmen. House owners who wanted a new mosaic would discuss the project with the craftsmen and choose a design from pattern books. The mosaic makers would then prepare a detailed plan, and only start work when they had the full approval of the client. There were two ways of working: direct and indirect. By the direct method, the craftsmen prepared the site to create a firm base of smooth mortar, then laid the tiles directly in place, fixing them with mortar and grouting the joints. By the indirect method, the mosaic was prefabricated in the workshop and installed in completed segments. In this case, the mosaic tiles were laid upside down on a piece of cloth bearing a reversed image of the design (or just the most complex sections of the mosaic). Then a layer of mortar was applied to the back of the tiles, and a sheet of backing cloth laid over it. When dry, the whole mosaic could be flipped over, and spaces between the tiles grouted with mortar. The mosaic could then be carried in one piece to the place where it was to be installed.

Below: A floor mosaic from the Roman city of Volubilis, in North Africa, depicts sea creatures in the popular black-and-white style.

Step 4: The rest of the mosaic is completed.

Christian Burial

In Christianity, life on Earth is preparation—and a testing ground—for the afterlife. Great emphasis was placed on burial, and tombs became shrines where the living could continue to pray for the well-being of the dead in the afterlife. Some elaborate stone sarcophagi were carved in high relief in the Roman style. The sarcophagus of Junius Bassus, a leading official in Rome, is dated to 359 CE, when Christianity had only recently become legal. The style can be compared to that of the Ludovisi Sarcophagus (see page 23), made a century before, but the subject matter and the tone is very different.

Left: The marble sarcophagus of Junius Bassus has been decorated with a series of biblical scenes.

Early Christian and Byzantine Art

Christianity began in the early years of the Roman Empire and gradually spread through the Roman world in the face of fierce persecution. By 313 CE it had become such a powerful force that Emperor Constantine decided to stop trying to suppress it, and in 380, under Emperor Theodosius, Christianity became the official religion of the Roman Empire. By this time, the Roman Empire had split into two halves: The West was still ruled from Rome, but the main center of power was in the East, ruled from the capital Byzantium, which had been renamed Constantinople (now Istanbul). When the Roman West collapsed in 476 under the pressure of "barbarian" invasions, the East survived, and in the 6th century it began to expand around the Mediterranean as the Byzantine Empire.

The Christian Context

The Roman Empire and Christianity form a single, continuous, intertwined history. Much of early Christian art borrowed directly from Roman traditions (and thus from Greek traditions) in painting, relief sculpture, and mosaics. The main difference was the subject matter. Christian art focused almost exclusively on stories from the Old and New Testaments, and the lives of Christian saints and martyrs.

There were two main aims: to beautify places of worship, and to illustrate the scriptures as a means of communicating the message and mystical wonder of Christianity.

Above: This sculpted ivory panel shows the Byzantine emperor Justinian (reigned 527–565) on horseback. A list of Frankish kings and officials on the reverse is a reminder that many of the "barbarians" who then controlled Europe were Christian.

THE BASILICA

For centuries, early Christians had to meet in secret. But after Christianity became officially tolerated in the Roman Empire, they could start building churches. An early model was large Roman meeting hall called a basilica, a feature of many forums. Christians adapted this form when they came to build their first places of worship. A basilica had a long central hall, which became the nave; interior colonnades, which became the aisles; a porch, which became the narthex, or entrance area; and sometimes a lateral building at the far end, which became the transept (representing the crosspiece of Christ's cross). These elements later became standard features for any large church.

Transept

Clerestory
(upper windows)

Nave

Side aisle

Narthex

Atrium

SHOWCASE: THE BATTLE OF DAVID AND GOLIATH

This is the largest of a set of nine silver plates illustrating scenes from the Old Testament story of King David. The plates were made in Constantinople in 629–630 CE and were found among a hoard of treasure in Cyprus in 1902. The plates may have been specially commissioned by the Byzantine emperor Heraclius (reigned 610–641) to celebrate his recent victory over the Persians and the recapture of Jerusalem. This campaign culminated in one-to-one combat between Heraclius and the Persian general Rhahzadh, in which Heraclius decapitated his opponent—an event that may well have inspired the theme of this plate. The composition is divided into three bands telling the story of the young David's unlikely victory over the mighty Philistine champion Goliath.

The main, central band shows the start of the conflict.

The combatants carry Roman-style weapons and armor.

The design of the embossed, low-relief images is in the style of classical Roman and Greek art.

The lower band shows David triumphantly chopping off Goliath's head.

The upper band shows David challenging Goliath.

Mosaics

The Byzantines used mosaics to stunning effect. Churches—such as those of Ravenna, Italy, built in the 5th and 6th century CE—often have fairly plain and modest exteriors, but inside they are awash with spectacular, glittering color. Biblical scenes and Christian images are combined with geometric patterns, often including large areas of gold and deep blue—all guaranteed to fill worshippers with a sense of awe and wonderment.

Left: A large, 13th-century mosaic over the altar at Monreale Cathedral, Sicily, depicts Christ giving his blessing.

Icons

Over the years, Christianity in the Byzantine Empire took a different course from the Christianity of Rome, resulting in the split, in 1054, between the Eastern Orthodox Church and the Roman Catholic Church. One of the causes of conflict was the role of religious images. While the Roman Catholic Church allowed statues of holy figures, the Orthodox Church focused on flat, painted portraits called icons (images) featuring only the head and upper body. These became the subject of passionate veneration. According to legend, St. Luke (patron saint of painters) created the first icon of the Madonna, but icons show many of the stylized characteristics seen in Roman portrait painting.

Above: The much-revered 12th-century Russian icon the Vladimir Virgin shows a Madonna and Child set against a background of gold.

Byzantine Architecture

Byzantine architecture was the first truly Christian architecture. It had much in common with Roman architecture, such as the semicircular arches and use of columns, but it developed its own, very distinctive style. One particularly recognizable feature is the mosaics used to decorate interior (and sometimes exterior) walls and ceilings. The Byzantines also made greater use of the dome. While in the West the ground plan of churches was in the shape of a crucifix, Byzantine basilicas took the form of the Greek cross, with the nave and transept of equal length.

Below: The Basilica of St. Mark in Venice, Italy, was built in classic Byzantine style between 978 and 1096 CE.

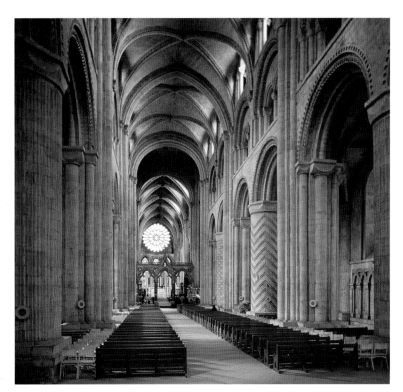

Above: The massive cylindrical columns and rounded arches in the nave of Durham Cathedral follow the Romanesque tradition.

THE BAPTISTERY, FLORENCE

The Baptistery of San Giovanni in Florence, Italy, stands just to the west of the Duomo (cathedral). It was designed as a place where the city's children could be baptised —because unbaptised children were not allowed inside the cathedral. It shows the strong influence of Roman architectural traditions in its arches and columns, and their precise, even, and symmetrical spacing. Its shape follows broadly the style of the Pantheon in Rome (see page 24), and the octagonal (eight-sided) Byzantine church of San Vitale in Ravenna, which dates to the 6th century CE. The octagon was often used for Christian buildings of this era: The number eight was believed to have sacred significance, symbolizing the seven days of creation, plus one for eternity. The existing baptistery was built in the 11th century and is also a symbol of the start of the development of Florence as a confident, independent, and prosperous republic.

Left: The exterior of the baptistery is elegantly faced in white and green marble.

England

The Normans, from northern France, conquered Britain in 1066 and brought with them not only greater stability, but also their traditions of building in stone. They built churches, cathedrals, and castles using the rounded arches of the Romanesque style (which in Britain is generally referred to as the Norman style). Durham Cathedral, in northern England, shows it at its best. Work began in 1093; the colossal nave was built after 1130. Many of the early Romanesque churches had barrel-vaulted roofs with a single long arch shaped like half a barrel; they tended to be dark, because large windows would weaken the walls bearing all the weight of the roof. In Durham Cathedral, a lighter roof structure was created by using stone ribs crossing diagonally. These are supported not by the walls but by the corner columns, permitting high windows to light up the nave.

France

France takes its name from the Franks, a Germanic people that swept into the old Roman province of Gaul in the 5th century and established an empire. Under Charlemagne (reigned 768–814), France became part of a large empire that included much of Germany and stretched as far south as Rome. This empire broke up after Charlemagne's death, and after 987, kings of the Capetian dynasty gradually took control of the whole of France. Meanwhile, the church in France grew in strength and confidence. Powerful monasteries, such as Cluny (founded in 909) and Cîteaux (1098), developed a network of monasteries across France and beyond, and promoted their style of Romanesque architecture, with ever more ambitious vaulted ceilings. This had a major influence on the many churches and cathedrals built during this era.

Romanesque Architecture

After the collapse of the Roman Empire in Italy in the 5th century CE, Western Europe went through a period of turmoil lasting about 500 years. The Roman Catholic Church was the only unifying force, with links right across Europe, communicating across borders in the old Roman language of Latin. When, after about 900, Europe became more stable, the cities began to prosper through trade. To demonstrate their new wealth and their devotion to religion, they began building grand churches and cathedrals. Architects created structures with the same kind of rounded arches that the Romans had used, and so the style that they used became known as Romanesque.

Below: The 11th-century west front of the Church of Notre Dame la Grande, in Poitiers, France, is decorated with sculpture of biblical figures set beneath the Romanesque arches.

SHOWCASE: THE PALATINE CHAPEL, AACHEN

Charlemagne saw himself as the emperor of a revived Roman Empire. He built on a grand, Roman-style scale at the capital of his empire, Aachen, in Germany. The only surviving building of this era is his Palatine (palace) Chapel. Built between 792 and 805, it followed the model of the Church of San Vitale in Ravenna. Yet this is very much a Romanesque building, dominated by its robust structure of arches.

The "westwork" includes towers with spiral staircases leading to a private chapel and the upper galleries.

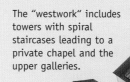

The marble columns in the arches are decorative only and have no structural function.

The emperor's marble throne stands in a gallery on the first floor, overlooking the main chapel.

Left: The octagonal chapel rises up through three stories to the dome. The proportions were based on 7, 12, and 14, which were considered sacred numbers from the Bible. The circular, Romanesque chandelier was donated by Emperor Friedrich Barbarossa in 1156.

Italy

Architects in Italy had their own Roman and Byzantine examples to inspire them, and in their hands the Romanesque style was light, sophisticated, and elegant. Following a Roman tradition, their buildings were faced with white marble, cut from the old Roman quarries of Carrara, offset by trimmings of darker marble. This effect was enhanced by the use of freestanding pillars, creating ranks of galleries on the outside of the buildings—a style brought to perfection in the cathedral complex (built between 1063 and 1350) at the thriving seaport of Pisa. Such buildings set a high standard of delicacy that was not matched by the rest of Europe until the era of Gothic architecture.

Below: The cross-shaped Cathedral of Pisa is best known for its separate campanile (bell tower), which began leaning even while it was being built.

Above: The Basilica of Sant'Ambrogio in Milan was built in the 11th and 12th centuries in the Romanesque style on foundations dating to the 4th century.

Illuminated Manuscripts

During these centuries of turmoil, knowledge and learning was preserved by the Christian Church. Books were handwritten, laboriously copied by monks onto sheets of parchment (animal skin). Many of these books were exquisitely illustrated (or "illuminated") with detailed drawings and designs, in ink, colored pigments, and gold leaf. They took hundreds of hours to complete, but for the monks who made them this was an act of religious devotion and worship. One of the greatest examples is the *Book of Kells*, containing selected passages from the Gospels; it was made by monks of the remote Scottish island of Iona in about 800, and taken to Ireland for safekeeping against Viking raids.

Above: Built like a jewelry casket and decorated with gilt figures and colored enamel, this 13th-century French reliquary was designed to contain the remains of saints.

Reliquaries

Throughout the medieval period, the Roman Catholic Church placed great emphasis on the sacred significance of holy relics. These were supposedly the remains of biblical figures or saints, such as the bones of saints, bits of Christ's cross, and even drops of Christ's blood. Many relics were said to have miraculous powers, which could bring rewards to anyone who prayed before them. Particularly famous relics became the focus of pilgrimages, with pilgrims traveling hundreds of miles to see them. Precious relics were kept in cases called reliquaries, and these were often works of exquisite craftsmanship, encrusted with jewels and with sculptures in silver and gold.

Above: This page from the Book of Kells *shows the* Chi-Rho *symbol, the letters that begin the word* Christ *in Greek. Winged angels and a face appear among the profusion of whirls and interlacing patterns that are typical of Celtic design.*

Early Medieval Arts

Right: Five wooden animal-headed posts were found at the ship burial of Oseberg, Norway. They may have played a part in rituals.

The 500 hundred years or so that followed the collapse of the Western Roman Empire are sometimes known as the Dark Ages. It was a period of confusion, invasions, and mass migration, when much of the stability and technical sophistication of the Roman Empire was lost. Germanic tribes filled the vacuum left by the retreating Romans: As the Franks moved into France, the Ostrogoths moved into Italy, and the Angles and Saxons moved into Britain. In the late 8th century, Viking warriors from Scandinavia, in their longships, began terrorizing the coasts of northern Europe. Despite this, the traditions of skilled art and craftsmanship thrived, building on the Roman traditions as well as developing new kinds of expression that reflected the times.

Viking Art

The Vikings came from Norway, Sweden, and Denmark—lands that had never been touched by the Roman world. They were notorious as raiders, but they were also explorers, traders, settlers, and skilled craftsmen. They made intricate jewelry, especially brooches, in bronze, silver, and gold, as well as stone sculpture.

Their distinctive approach to art can be seen particularly in their wood carving: Relief carvings of interlacing geometric patterns and figures decorate their ships, sleds, carts, furniture, and board games. Many Viking treasures have been found in their elaborate burials, which sometimes included whole ships.

Above: Most medieval sculptors are unnamed, but a sculptor called Wiligelmo is known to have worked at the Modena Cathedral in Italy during the 12th century. Here a piece of decorative stonework illustrates the idea that upside-down people, called the Antipodes, live on the opposite side of the world.

Romanesque Stone Carving

Romanesque churches, particularly in France, are noted for their lavish and intense sculpture. This is found particularly in the capitals at the tops of columns, and in the semicircular area, called a tympanum, between the top of a doorway and the arch. The subjects could vary from biblical stories to pagan myths, and included signs of the zodiac, monsters and hybrid creatures, and naked figures writhing in hell.

They were carved in deep relief in the manner of Greek and Roman sculpture, but on a smaller a scale and with greater freedom and imaginative invention, providing a sense of intensely busy activity, often spiced with earthy touches of humor. Such sculptures would have been painted, providing vivid illustrations of religious teachings, especially for the many members of the public who could not read.

Above: A 12th-century tympanum at the Basilica of Sainte Madeleine, in Vézelay, France, shows a seated Christ in the center dispatching his apostles to teach the faith to foreign peoples represented in the eight panels above them. Below, on the lintel above the door, undiscovered pagan peoples gather toward Christ.

SHOWCASE: THE BAYEUX TAPESTRY

The Normans were descended from Vikings (Northmen) who settled in northern France. In 1066 Duke William of Normandy conquered England in pursuit of his claim to the throne. The story of the critical Battle of Hastings is celebrated in the Bayeux Tapestry, made shortly after 1066. It is not in fact a true tapestry, but a strip of embroidered linen; measuring 230 feet (70 m) long, for centuries it hung in the cathedral of Bayeux, in Normandy.

The story is told in 79 scenes. Here the English infantry comes under attack from the French cavalry, close to the start of the battle.

The top band is decorated with animals, both real and fanciful. The lower band shows the dead and injured.

Eight colors of woolen thread were used: three blues, two greens, yellow, red, and grey.

Italian Gothic

In northern Europe, the Gothic style became highly visible, showcased in magnificent cathedrals and countless churches, many of which were designed and built in pure Gothic style. In Italy, Gothic architecture arrived with the Cistercians (from the French abbey of Cîteaux) and was seen in its purest form only in their monasteries. Elsewhere, it appears more in details than in whole structures. Windows, for instance, are broken up into sets of two or three long shapes (lancet windows) divided by delicate columns. The vaulted ceilings of churches meet under pointed arches. Instead of thick, round Romanesque columns, structural columns were made up of clusters of pillars. The effect was to add a lighter touch to architectural design and put more emphasis on vertical shapes.

Left: The elected leader of the wealthy island-city of Venice was called the doge. His 12th-century residence, and the seat of government, was the splendid Gothic-style Palazzo Ducale, standing between the Basilica of St. Mark (see page 29) and the waterfront.

Gothic Architecture

Right: Designed by the painter Giotto di Bondone (c. 1266–1337), the 14th-century cathedral bell tower of Florence stands apart from the main building.

The most distinctive feature of the next phase of building design, Gothic architecture, is the pointed arch. A pointed arch is not as strong, structurally, as the rounded arch of Romanesque architecture, but it is more elegant. The pointed arch was something new to Europe, although it had been used in Islamic architecture. It had no connection to ancient Rome—and for this reason the Christian Church liked it; it represented a clear break from the pagan past. However, the term *Gothic* was actually coined later by art critics who loved everything Roman, and they saw this departure from the Roman (and Romanesque) model as the equivalent of the destruction of the Roman civilization by the "barbarian" Goths. It was intended as an insult.

Left: Flagged by its magnificent bell tower, the Palazzo Pubblico ("Public Palace," or town hall) of Siena was built in 1288–1309. It stands in the center of the city, beside the main market square.

Bell Towers

The sound of bells became a symbol of Western Christian civilization. In Italy there was a tradition of building cathedral bell towers (*campanili*) as separate structures. They served to call the faithful to prayer, to announce the passing hours, and to raise the alarm in an emergency. Civilian bell towers served similar purposes. They became city landmarks and the object of great civic pride.

Civic Buildings

As Europe began to prosper through trade, the cities became the main focus of human activity, with markets, craftsmen's workshops and guilds, merchants, tax authorities, and government administrators. This represented a shift of power away from the castles of dukes and princes. Many cities resembled small independent or semi-independent states, with their own governments. They took pride in their town halls, the symbols of their independent authority. In Italy, many of these were designed in a style that combined the traditions of castle building with the new Gothic style.

Gothic Cathedrals

In northern Europe, cathedrals became the great prestige buildings of the cities. Gothic design was based on a strong structural skeleton, with the weight of the roof taken by pillars reinforced by buttresses outside the building. This meant that the walls, freed from the task of load-bearing, could be filled with windows, permitting light—often colored by stained glass—to fill the interior like a lantern. The great Gothic cathedrals were huge projects, taking decades to complete and involving thousands of laborers and craftsmen, many of whom considered their work to be an act of worship. Driven by competition with rival cities, the architects pushed the boundaries of technical know-how to the limits, which sometimes resulted in structural collapse.

Left: The interior of King's College Chapel in Cambridge, England, built 1446–1515, demonstrates the exceptional delicacy of late Gothic style.

Right: The more robust style of earlier Gothic can be seen in the facade of Notre Dame, the cathedral of Paris, built 1163–1345.

SHOWCASE: CATHEDRAL OF NOTRE DAME, CHARTRES

The Cathedral of Notre Dame in Chartres, in northern France, is remarkable for many reasons. Despite its huge scale, most of it was built in just 25 years at the start of the 13th century. As a result, apart from the spires, its Gothic style is unusually uniform. The builders made full use of the structural advantage of Gothic architecture to fill the walls with stained-glass windows—176 of them, most of which are still the originals. The cathedral is dedicated to the Virgin Mary (*Notre Dame*, "Our Lady"), and its most treasured possession is a piece of cloth said to come from her robe when she gave birth to Jesus, a major focus of pilgrimage.

The lacy North Tower was built in late Flamboyant Gothic style in 1507–13, after fire destroyed an earlier wooden spire.

The three windows below the rose window date from the earlier Romanesque cathedral and contain a distinctive blue glass that has given rise to the term *Chartres blue*.

The 12th-century South Tower, or Old Bell Tower, is one of the few remnants of the earlier Romanesque cathedral, which burned down in 1194.

The ribs on columns in the nave rise up directly to form the rib structure of the ceiling vault, 126 feet (36 m) above the ground.

The pitched roof was covered in copper in the 19th century, hence its green oxidized color.

Large round windows of stained glass (called rose windows) fill the upper part of each of the cathedral fronts.

Triple entrances, or portals, have been placed not only on the west front, but also at each end of the transept. All the portals are richly decorated with sculpture depicting scenes from the Bible.

Buttresses around the exterior reinforce the whole structure without affecting the interior space. Some of these are "flying buttresses"—freestanding pillars connected to the building by arches.

A ground plan of the cathedral
1. Towers
2. Narthex
3. Nave
4. Aisles
5. Transept
6. Choir
7. Ambulatory
8. Chapels

Right: A drawing of the nave walls shows how they are divided into three elements. The greater strength at the base gives way to the lighter structure of the upper windows, supporting a larger area of glass, reinforced by a gallery between the two.

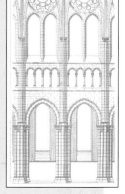

Gothic Arts

In the two centuries between about 1050 and 1350, the art of Western Europe evolved rapidly. The church remained the primary patron of the arts, and virtually all art was made for religious purposes. Cathedrals, churches, and chapels were filled with sculptures, paintings, and stained glass, becoming dazzling monuments to spiritual devotion, and to the power of the church. Over time, Gothic art lost the earthy and crude vigor that enlivened and distinguished early medieval work. Instead a greater technical skill was applied to produce images that were more realistic and polished, and generally calmer in tone. This can be seen particularly in sculpture, where the practitioners were clearly beginning to admire the work of Roman sculptors and to analyze how they had achieved such high standards of representation. Naturally, this was easiest for sculptors in Italy, which had by far the most Roman remains.

Above: The great rose window of the north transept of Chartres Cathedral (see page 35) illustrates the Virgin Mary holding baby Jesus (in the center), surrounded by angels, doves, kings of Israel, and the prophets.

Stained Glass

The world's earliest stained-glass windows are found in Augsburg Cathedral in Germany, and date from about 1065, in the Romanesque era. It was the Gothic era, however, that brought the art of stained glass to perfection, exploiting the opportunities for large window areas that Gothic architecture provided. The total area of stained glass in Chartres Cathedral, for instance, amounts to the equivalent of more than seven tennis courts. Stained-glass windows are designed rather like mosaics; pieces of colored glass make up the pictures. The glass was clipped out of large sheets into the desired shape, assembled on a table, then stuck together with strips of lead. Finer details of the picture (such as faces) were painted onto the glass in dark enamel paint, then fired in a kiln before assembly. In churches, the pictures often illustrate stories from the Bible, and might also include portraits or references to whoever paid for the window, such as wealthy private individuals, or tradesmen's guilds.

Sculpture in Italy

Italian sculpture took a new direction in the 13th century, led in particular by Nicola Pisano (c. 1220–c.1284). In his earliest known work, the marble pulpit (dating to about 1260) in the Baptistery of Pisa, he created large and complex pictures in high relief depicting various scenes from the life of Christ. In style, these recall the kind of high-relief sculpture seen in Roman sarcophagi (see page 23), which Pisano would have seen at Pisa. Effectively, he has turned images of Roman gods and heroes into Christ and the saints, but imbued them with emotion and humanity. Nicola Pisano abandoned the Romanesque tradition of breaking the panels up into bands (see the tympanum on page 33) in favor of a more single-minded form of composition. He also introduced to Italy the northern European Romanesque habit of incorporating statues into architecture. His son Giovanni (died after 1314) maintained this tradition, creating sculpture for his sumptuous facade of the Cathedral of Siena. Another key sculptor of the time was Andrea Pisano (c. 1290–1348; of no relation to the others), who worked in Florence and designed the relief sculptures for the first set of bronze doors for the baptistery (see page 30).

Right: A bas-relief (low relief) sculpture depicting God's creation of Adam, by Andrea Pisano, forms part of the decoration of the base of the bell tower of Florence's cathedral (see page 34).

Below: Nicola Pisano's marble pulpit in the Baptistery of Pisa shows six scenes from the life of Christ. Here (nearest), the presentation of baby Jesus at the temple.

Gothic Sculpture in Northern Europe

The church connections that spanned Europe permitted the rapid exchange of ideas about art and architecture. Sophisticated Gothic sculpture was soon found in all parts. In the case of northern European cathedral building, many of the architects were also stone masons by trade, and so it was only natural that they thought of decoration in terms of sculpture, which—as in previous times—would have been painted. Sculptural detail became more uniform, disciplined, and stylized than it had been in Romanesque times, but there were also exceptional pieces of unique individuality, such as *The Bamberg Horseman*. Dating to about 1235, it was the first large-scale equestrian statue since the Roman era.

Left: The Bamberg Horseman *is the most famous sculpture among an impressive collection in Bamberg Cathedral, Germany. Neither the sculptor nor the subject of this statue is known for certain.*

SHOWCASE: REIMS CATHEDRAL, *THE ANNUNCIATION AND THE VISITATION*

The exteriors of many northern European cathedrals were adorned with sculpture, usually depicting biblical figures and the saints. Portals (entrances) sometimes contain ranks of stone figures. These were usually attached to the stonework, but in the west portal at Reims Cathedral in northern France, carved in about 1225–45, the sculptures are completely detached from the walls. Four figures represent two scenes: The Annunciation to the Virgin Mary (the two figures on the left), in which the angel Gabriel announces to Mary the future birth of her son Jesus, and the Visitation (right), showing Mary visiting her cousin St. Elizabeth, future mother of St. John the Baptist.

Gold Sculpture

Naturalistic sculpture also extended to small-scale work in gold and other metals. Gold-work formed an important part of many artists' studios, where a number of artists and apprentices would work under the command of a master, producing jewelry and church treasures as well as paintings and sculpture. Gold statues were cast using the lost wax process (see page 18). They were usually commissioned for religious purposes. Patrons— the people who commissioned art and paid for it—would order statues to donate to a church as an act of worship, or as penance to pay for some wrongdoing. The subjects during this period were almost always figures from the Bible, particularly the Virgin Mary with the baby Jesus (Virgin and Child).

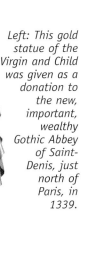

Left: This gold statue of the Virgin and Child was given as a donation to the new, important, wealthy Gothic Abbey of Saint-Denis, just north of Paris, in 1339.

In sharp contrast to Romanesque sculpture, the poses of the four figures are naturalistic and well observed.

The two portraits of Mary differ in a significant number of ways, indicating that they were carved by different sculptors. The angel appears to have been carved by a third sculptor.

The folds in the garments of the right-hand figures (the Visitation) suggest that the sculptor had studied Roman statues.

At the Visitation, St. Elizabeth was six months pregnant, and there is some discreet indication of this.

Duccio

Duccio di Buoninsegna (c. 1260–1319) was a key figure in the development of painting in Siena. As with Cimabue, Duccio's work was heavily influenced by Byzantine traditions, but he brought to these a new sense of emotion and drama. However, whereas Cimabue's work in Florence led to Giotto and much greater freedoms and invention in composition, the Sienese style remained closer to the traditions of Byzantine and Gothic art. Duccio was a lively character, often in dispute with the authorities in Siena. But he was also highly successful, and achieved considerable wealth and fame. His great *Maestà* painting was apparently carried from his studio to the cathedral in a triumphant procession.

Right: Duccio's Maestà *also included 26 panels on the back depicting scenes from the Bible. Here,* Christ Washing the Feet of His Disciples.

This large crucifix, attributed to Cimabue, hangs in the nave of the Church of Santa Croce in Florence. It has been restored since it was badly damaged by floods that devastated Florence in 1966.

Cimabue

Cenni di Pepi (c. 1240–1302) is better known to us as Cimabue, a nickname meaning "ox head." (Many artists of this era went by one-word names.) Very little is known about his life, and it is not totally clear which paintings were by him: At this time, paintings were created by studios using a number of artists and were unsigned. However, it seems likely that Cimabue was responsible for very beautiful religious paintings in the Byzantine style, sparkling with gold leaf and full of compassion. Based in Florence, Cimabue may have taught Giotto; certainly the beginning of a freer, three-dimensional style can be detected in the work attributed to him.

SHOWCASE: *THE MADONNA AND CHILD ENTHRONED*

In Italian Gothic art, a traditional subject for altarpieces was the Virgin Mary, seated with the baby Jesus on her knee, surrounded by adoring angels. Such paintings are usually called *The Madonna and Child Enthroned*, and sometimes *Maestà* (the Italian for "majesty"). Mary, the Madonna, occupied a place in medieval Christianity that was almost as sacred as that of Christ himself, and such paintings were designed to inspire meditation and wonderment. These three examples, all now in the Uffizi Gallery in Florence, show how the artists respected the conventions on the one hand, but expressed their individuality on the other.

Below: Cimabue's version, Madonna Enthroned with Angels and Prophets, *was painted in about 1280–90 for the high altar of the Santa Trinità Church in Florence.*

A feature of a *Maestà* was the background of gold leaf, a tradition that connects directly with Byzantine traditions. Gold leaf is also used for the halos, an artistic convention used to signify the radiating light of holiness.

To modern eyes the child figures in such paintings are rarely convincing: Their features and proportions make them look neither quite like babies nor infants.

In some *Maestà* paintings, saints and other exalted holy figures appear, as well as angels.

As in Byzantine icons (see page 29), the Madonna has her head covered with a round, dark veil. Only Giotto's version shows a more contemporary kind of veil.

Cimabue, Duccio, and Giotto

Gothic sophistication also spread to painting. This was one of the great art forms of Italy. Churches, town halls, and palaces were decorated with frescoed wall paintings, while chapels and altars focused on exquisite devotional pictures delicately painted on wooden panels in layers of egg-based tempera. Early religious paintings, particularly from Tuscany, had much in common with Byzantine icons (see page 29). But the more naturalistic scenes depicted by Giotto soon brought about a dramatic change in attitudes toward painting.

Giotto

Giotto di Bondone (c. 1266–1337) is seen as the first significant artist to break away from the conventions of Byzantine art. Giotto brought to art a new sense of three-dimensional reality. Perhaps learning from the kind of scene depiction found in illuminated manuscripts and relief sculpture, he told stories with his art, introducing emotional drama to his scenes, which he filled with figures that possess individuality. He achieved all this even when using the difficult medium of fresco, wall painting that involved working quickly on damp plaster. By comparison, the Byzantine tradition looks stylized and limiting. This shift was recognized at the time: In his great work *The Divine Comedy*, the Italian poet Dante (1265–1321) records that Giotto's fame eclipsed that of Cimabue, and it made him both very successful and rich.

All the paintings have the same tall format and are painted in egg-based tempera on wooden panels.

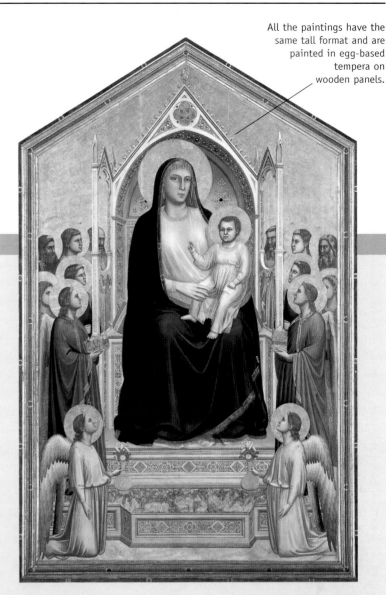

Above: Giotto's version, The Ognissanti Madonna, *was painted in about 1305–10 for the Ognissanti (All Saints') Church in Florence. Here prominence is given to the saints, who, despite the halos and the presence of angels, are clearly connected to life on Earth.*

Above: Duccio's version, The Rucellai Madonna, *painted in 1285, was commissioned for the Rucellai family chapel in the Santa Maria Novella Church in Florence—despite the fact that Florence and Siena (Duccio's hometown) were bitter enemies.*

The painting has a very formal, structured composition, with angels evenly distributed on either side, but this also helps to give it great calm and poise.

GIOTTO AND THE ORIGINS OF RENAISSANCE PAINTING

Many aspects of Giotto's art were well in advance of their time. His figures have the weight and robust volume of sculpture. Indeed, it is likely that he studied the relief sculptures on Roman sarcophagi. He had a gift for describing the gestures and expressions of daily life. Many of Giotto's faces resemble portraits. Giotto's frescoes, which fill the walls of the Basilica of St. Francis in Assisi would be a kind of school for the Renaissance in the next century. The early Renaissance painter Masaccio (see page 46) was so inspired by these qualities that scholars have called him "Giotto reborn."

Right: A detail from The Mourning of St. Francis *shows how Giotto introduced a sense of depth and individual character into his work.*

The Wilton Diptych

This small painting was made as a portable altarpiece, perhaps for the private devotion of the young King Richard II, who came to the throne of England at the age of 10 in 1377 and ruled until 1399. It consists of two hinged panels (diptych), which could be folded together and easily carried. The painting presents the kind of crisp, polished detail that sets International Gothic painting apart. The artist is unknown—as is the case with many medieval paintings—but it probably dates to about 1395.

Left: The left-hand panel of The Wilton Diptych *shows Richard II, as a boy, being presented by his patron saint John the Baptist, with Saints Edward and Edmund, to (in the right-hand panel) the Virgin Mary and baby Jesus.*

Above: The Dutch sculptor Claus Sluter (c. 1350–1406) mixed a new sense of monumental grandeur with a close observation of naturalistic detail, as seen in this group called The Well of Moses, *at Dijon, France.*

International Gothic

By the end of the 14th century, Gothic art had achieved a new level of sophistication. Pictures in illuminated manuscripts display great technical skill. Other artists borrowed from that tradition to produce large-scale paintings filled with intricate, naturalistic detail and vivid color, with an almost jewel-like intensity. The style developed in both Italy and France and through contacts between artists from both regions, and it soon spread right across Europe, lasting well into the 15th century. It also had a parallel effect on European sculpture.

Above: In The Annunciation and Two Saints, *painted by Simone Martini in 1333, the gilded beauty of Byzantine art combines with the fine detail and emotional intensity of International Gothic.*

Simone Martini

Siena's greatest Sienese artist after Duccio—and perhaps his pupil—was Simone Martini (c. 1285–1344). In his earlier works he shows signs of both the refined elegance and aloofness of the earlier Byzantine style, as well as the ravishing, gracious beauty of the Gothic style that was fashionable in Siena during his lifetime. His work was highly appreciated in France, and he spent the final years of his life in Avignon, then the home of the popes; as a result, he had a major influence on the International Gothic style in France.

Above: Gentile da Fabriano's greatest surviving work, The Adoration of the Magi *(1423), was commissioned by the wealthy merchant Palla Strozzi as an altarpiece for Santa Trinità Church in Florence.*

Gentile da Fabriano

The Italian artist Gentile da Fabriano (c. 1370–1427) painted many significant works in important centers of art across Italy. Unfortunately most of them have been lost. They included frescoes in the Palazzo Ducale in Venice (see page 34) and in the Church of St. John the Baptist in Rome. In the works that do still exist, the rich coloring, fine detail, and naturalistic rendering all suggest that he was perhaps the greatest exponent of the International Gothic style in Italy. He certainly had a major influence on a number of important Italian artists of the next generation. However, his dazzling surface texture of brilliant detail comes at the expense of the drama of the moment portrayed.

SHOWCASE: THE LIMBOURG BROTHERS, *LES TRÈS RICHES HEURES DU DUC DE BERRY*

Book illumination was one of the greatest art forms of the medieval world. The illustrations, in minuscule detail and vibrantly colored, covered all subjects, from biblical scenes to daily life. Skills in book illumination reached new heights in the early 15th century with three Dutch brothers: Paul, Johan, and Herman Limbourg. Their most celebrated work was a book of hours, a kind of illustrated book of prayers for the passing hours, accompanied by a calendar. It was produced for Duke Jean de Berry in 1413–16 and includes much about his real life. The book was unfinished when all three Limbourg brothers died in 1416, probably the victims of plague.

This painting is one of twelve full-page illustrations representing the months. This is January, which, at the time, was the month for exchanging gifts. It is painted on vellum (calfskin parchment).

A silk canopy over the fireplace is decorated with the duke's heraldic symbols.

Battling knights are pictured on the tapestry hanging on the wall.

Duke Jean de Berry is portrayed seated in a brilliant blue robe and a fur hat.

The crowded figures behind the table appear to occupy a realistic space.

The exquisite detail includes the table laid with dishes of food on fine platters, and a gold saltcellar—often the most precious piece of tableware—in the shape of a ship.

Ambrogio and Pietro Lorenzetti

Little is known about the lives of these two brothers, but they were painting in Siena from about 1319 to 1348, when both may have died, perhaps of plague. Ambrogio was the most innovative of the two: His pair of frescoes representing *The Effects of Good and Bad Government*, in the town hall at Siena (see page 34), shows a bold new approach to landscape and crowd scenes. Pietro's work was more emotionally expressive, and he is remembered especially for the dramatic power of his fresco *Descent from the Cross* at Assisi.

Below: In his Effects of Good Government, *Ambrogio Lorenzetti depicts a harmonious medieval Italian city.*

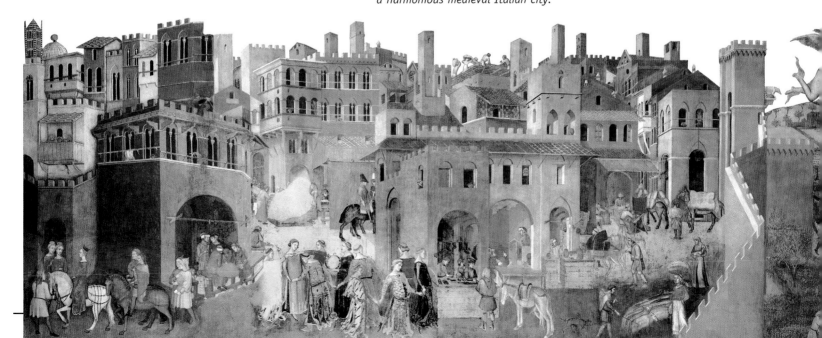

Early Renaissance
Architecture in Italy

Renaissance means "rebirth" and is a term applied to a great shift in art, learning, and attitudes over two centuries from about 1350, first in Italy, then elsewhere in Europe. A new freedom of individual inquiry, lacking in the Middle Ages, was in the air. This spirit was personified in architecture by Filippo Brunelleschi (1377–1446), the first artist in history to go to Rome in order to study the ruins in the Forum. His new style was a geometric arrangement of classical columns and arches. At the heart of this movement was the city of Florence. Wealthy and ambitious, it was ruled by people, notably the Medici family, with a genuine interest in artistic innovation. When Cosimo de' Medici died in 1464, he said his only regret was that he had not constructed more buildings, for architecture is the most enduring of the arts.

Above: Michelozzo's library at the convent of San Marco, Florence, is now aptly used to house an exhibition of manuscript illumination.

Below: Alberti designed the Palazzo Rucellai for one of the leading merchant families in Florence. It was built between 1446 and 1451.

Michelozzo

Michelozzo di Bartolomeo (1396–1472) started his career as a sculptor, working alongside several of the great masters of Florentine sculpture, notably Ghiberti and Donatello (see pages 44–45). He turned to architecture later in life, and in 1444 he was commissioned by Cosimo de' Medici (ruler of Florence 1434–64) to design a palace for his family, the Palazzo Medici Riccardi, a robust town mansion built around an inner courtyard. On the outside of this building, Michelozzo used a roughened kind of stonework called rustication, which soon became the fashion for the exteriors of grand palaces (seen, for example, on Alberti's Palazzo Rucellai, left). Michelozzo strikes a more delicate note with his cloister at the Dominican convent of San Marco, and the library (c. 1440) on the upper floor—next to the cells of the monks' dormitory famously decorated with wall paintings by Fra Angelico (c. 1387–1455). The influence of Roman models can be seen in the rounded (as opposed to Gothic) arches and the elegant proportions and spacing.

Alberti

Born in Genoa, Leon Battista Alberti (1404–72) went to Florence in about 1428 and quickly joined a circle that included many of the leading artists, sculptors, and architects of the Florentine Renaissance. He too was multitalented, not only an architect but also a painter, sculptor, and writer, and—using this combination—one of the most important theorists about art and architecture of his day. He laid strong emphasis on the mathematical basis of architecture, which can be seen in the symmetry and proportions of his churches and palaces in Florence and the other northern Italian cities where he worked. He was also one of the first Renaissance architects to consider the concept of integrated and unified urban planning schemes.

Right: The facade of the Church of Santa Maria Novella, Florence, exemplifies the elegant poise of Alberti's mathematical principles.

SHOWCASE: BRUNELLESCHI, THE PAZZI CHAPEL

Filippo Brunelleschi was the first and most celebrated of all the great Florentine Renaissance architects. With the chapel that he designed in about 1440 for the Pazzi family at the basilica in Santa Croce, Florence, he reveals his ability to adapt antique forms to the needs of a Christian sanctuary. The simple, elegant proportions of the Pazzi Chapel reflect the Renaissance ideal of religion that celebrates the supreme lucidity of the mind of God.

Right: Mauro Coducci completed the facade of the Church of San Zaccaria in Venice— begun by another architect—in Renaissance style.

Below: Brunelleschi achieved an air of harmony and serenity in the interior. Every part of the plan is based upon precisely calculated measurements and proportions.

The exterior shows an interplay of ideal geometry. The chapel is designed as a cube surmounted by a circular dome.

The fluted pilasters are topped with classical-style Corinthian capitals.

Architecture in Venice

Renaissance architecture came relatively late to Venice, a unique island-city of canals that always had its own outlook on the world. The sculptor and architect Pietro Lombardo (c. 1435–1515) is credited with bringing the ideas of the Florentine Renaissance to the city. He demonstrated them to perfection with his Church of Maria dei Miracoli (1481–89), which has much in common with the Pazzi Chapel. Mauro Coducci (or Codussi; c. 1440–1504) worked in a similarly refined Renaissance style. This new look was captured by Venetian artists of the time, such as Giovanni Bellini (c. 1430–1516) and Vittore Carpaccio (c. 1460–1526).

Religious illustration is restricted to the 12 roundels, of blue and white glazed terra-cotta, depicting seated apostles, by Luca della Robbia, and four multicolored roundels of the evangelists.

Even the slabs of marble flooring have been carefully cut to conform to the mathematical proportions of the whole.

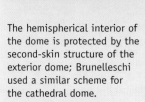

Below: Brunelleschi was famous above all for his cathedral dome(1420–36), an engineering triumph that still crowns the skyline of Florence.

The hemispherical interior of the dome is protected by the second-skin structure of the exterior dome; Brunelleschi used a similar scheme for the cathedral dome.

All proportions of the interior are based on cubes and hemispheres.

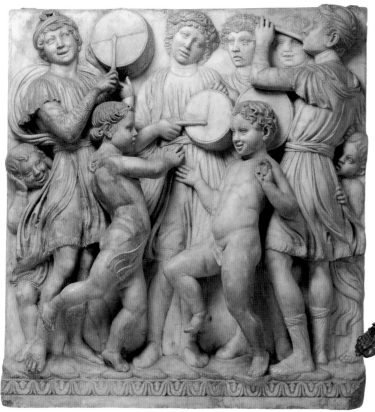

Andrea del Verrocchio

Andrea del Verrocchio (c. 1435–88) was a gifted draftsman, painter, and goldsmith, as well as a sculptor. He sculpted in marble and clay but is best known for his work in bronze. He may have trained under Donatello, and he produced both a *David* and an equestrian statue to rival his master, as well as religious pieces and portrait busts. Verrocchio ran one of the most successful studios in Florence: This is where Leonardo da Vinci began his training, at about age 17, in around 1469.

Left: Verrocchio's bronze Incredulity of St. Thomas *(1466–83) depicts the saint still hesitant with doubt before the resurrected Christ.*

Above: The engaging charm of Luca della Robbia's sculpture can be seen in his series of marble reliefs called Cantoria (Singing Gallery, 1431–8).

Luca della Robbia

The plaques of glazed terra-cotta, sculpted with relief images, that decorate many of the grander buildings, such as the Pazzi Chapel (see page 43) are notable features of the Renaissance cities of northern Italy. The leading creator of these was the Florentine sculptor Luca della Robbia (c. 1400–82). In his busy studio, he worked alongside his nephew Andrea (1435–1525), who continued with his sons after Luca's death.

Early Renaissance
Sculpture in Florence

Renaissance sculptors enjoyed an advantage over their fellow painters since numerous marbles and bronzes survived from antiquity, while no paintings did, apart from wall decorations. More and more Roman statues and coins were being unearthed all the time. These works set a very high standard for Renaissance sculptors, and many were up to the challenge. They strove to acquire the ancient artists' gift for making the human anatomy appear beautiful. In time, as part of the Renaissance enthusiasm for antiquity, artists provided their patrons with subjects and scenes taken from Roman and Greek myths. The rulers of the Italian city-states commissioned equestrian statues for display in public squares. The rise of a prosperous citizenry led to the revival of sculpted portraits for display in family residences and on tombs. Most of the sculpture produced in the period was destined for display in chapels or churches.

Donatello

Donato di Niccolò di Betto Bardi (1386–1466), known as Donatello, was the greatest sculptor of the early Renaissance, talented in every medium: bronze, stone, clay, and wood, in relief and in the round. He was a close friend of all the leading artists of Florence of his day. He traveled to Rome to study antique remains there. On his return he produced one of his most famous pieces, a bronze sculpture called the *David* (the slayer of Goliath)—but it has been suggested that it could actually depict the Roman god Mercury with the head of the slain herdsman Argus. It was the first free-standing nude since Roman times. In 1443–53 Donatello was in Padua, working on the first life-size equestrian statue since antiquity in Italy, the Gattamelata Monument. What set Donatello apart was his ability to inject his sculptures with the sense that they represented real, believable, living human beings caught in the emotion of the moment—something else that had not been achieved since Roman times.

Right: Donatello's David *is life-size and captures the figure in a naturalistic, slightly twisted pose called* contrapposto.

SHOWCASE: LORENZO GHIBERTI, *THE GATES OF PARADISE*

Lorenzo Ghiberti (1378–1455) spent most of his career working on two sets of elaborate gilded-bronze doors for the Baptistery of Florence (see page 30). Having finished the first, the North Door (1403–24), he was asked to do another set for the East Door, which took until 1452 to complete. To produce them, Ghiberti ran a busy studio, employing many of the best sculptors and artists of the day. Later, the great sculptor Michelangelo (see pages 50–51) declared that the second pair of doors was fit to be the Gates of Paradise, and that name has stuck.

The rules of perspective have been rigorously applied to the elaborate classical-style architecture in the background. The scene depicting Joseph in Egypt even contains a round building, which is particularly difficult to draw in perspective.

All the scenes are depicted to the same scale: The foreground figures are the same size throughout.

The soldiers watching David behead Goliath are dressed like Romans.

1	2
3	4
5	6
7	8
9	10

The doors feature 10 large panels in low relief depicting scenes of the Old Testament of the Bible: 1. Adam and Eve; 2. Cain and Abel; 3. Noah; 4. Abraham and the sacrifice of Isaac; 5. Isaac with Esau and Jacob; 6. Joseph in Egypt; 7. Moses receiving the Ten Commandments; 8. Joshua and the Fall of Jericho; 9. David and Goliath; 10. Solomon and the queen of Sheba.

The panels are remarkable for their detail. The figures strike naturalistic poses in complex compositions that would be a challenge even in painting, let alone cast in bronze.

The door frame contains statuettes of prophets and sibyls (prophetesses).

Above: Brunelleschi submitted this version of the sacrifice of Isaac to the competition.

The Competition for the Baptistery Doors

In 1401 seven selected Florentine sculptors were invited by a wealthy merchants' guild to submit entries for a competition to see who was best-suited to win a prestigious commission: the chance to design the panels for a new pair of bronze doors for the famous Baptistery. They all had to work in the same format—within the shape of a Gothic frame. The chosen subject was Abraham's sacrifice of Isaac, at the moment when he was prevented from killing his own son by the divine intervention of an angel. This was the first public art competition ever held, and it caused intense excitement in Florence. Among the contestants were Lorenzo Ghiberti and Filippo Brunelleschi. Ghiberti won: His design had a clarity, simplicity, and dynamism that permits the eye to roam around the composition. It is said that Brunelleschi was so disheartened by this experience that he thereafter all but abandoned sculpture to pursue architecture. Coming right at the very start of the 15th century, the event provided a major landmark in the history of Renaissance art.

Above: This bronze plaque depicting the sacrifice of Isaac, by Ghiberti, won the competition to make the first set of bronze doors for the baptistery.

Perspective

Many artists of the past had observed that objects appear smaller in the distance, and that parallel lines of architecture seem to converge as they lead toward the background. The technique of imitating this recession into the distance is known as perspective. With linear perspective, all parallel lines in a picture converge at a single vanishing point. The architect Filippo Brunelleschi (see pages 42–43) is credited with discovering the mathematical rules that govern how this works. Many artists, such as Piero della Francesca (1415–92), applied them rigorously to their paintings, sometimes allowing their obsession with this newfound "science" to dominate their work.

Above: A line drawing shows how, as parallel lines recede toward the vanishing point, objects become proportionally smaller relative to their distance from the viewer.

Left: The eerie tranquillity of Piero della Francesca's Flagellation of Christ *(1455) is reinforced by the meticulous perspective of the classical architecture.*

Early Renaissance
Painting in Italy

For Early Renaissance painters, picturing the world was a way of exploring its inner workings. The brightest and most creative talents—Masaccio, Fra Angelico, Piero della Francesca, Andrea Mantegna, Leonardo da Vinci, and Botticelli—spearheaded the investigation of anatomy, perspective, natural science, psychology, and theology. Masaccio's Brancacci Chapel was the first great burst of humanist optimism; it inaugurated a generation of painters who surpassed the limits of their own age. Christopher Columbus's discovery of continents was paralleled by their revelation of humanity's full dimension. Poets, philosophers, and artists shared their ideas at the noble courts of Florence, Urbino, Mantua, Venice, and Milan.

Masaccio

Tommaso di Ser Giovanni di Mone Cassai (1401–28), better known as Masaccio, is remembered particularly for his paintings in the Brancacci Chapel in Santa Maria del Carmine, Florence. Masaccio and Masolino (1383–1440), his respected senior partner, took turns frescoing the events in St. Peter's life, working their way down from the vault. The walls of the Brancacci Chapel are a coded message that compares the apostle's story to the history of the world, which finds its culmination in the thriving, stylish, rambunctious streets of Florence. In these, Masaccio shows a powerful, almost sculptural command of space, using consistent shadows, as well an ability to give his figures a believable emotional response to the dramas in which they are portrayed. Masaccio was a master of one-point perspective, influenced by Brunelleschi. Masaccio died in his late twenties, yet his brief career had a major impact on the history of painting.

Left: Masaccio captures the anguish of Adam and Eve in his Expulsion from Paradise, *from the Brancacci Chapel in Florence.*

Paolo Uccello

Paolo di Dono (c. 1397–1475), know as Uccello, was a devoted and obsessive painter, famous for his fixation with detail, as well as the rather unreal, fairy-tale mood of his work. This applies to his *Battle of San Romano*, created in three small panels (now each in separate museums) for the Palazzo Medici in Florence. In his detail, Uccello's work recalls the International Gothic, but he is clearly a Renaissance painter in his nonreligious subject matter, and his obsession with vanishing-point perspective—which he quite wrongly applies even to random objects, like fallen lances and battlefield casualties. *The Battle of San Romano* is painted in tempera on wooden panels, but Uccello also painted frescoes, and in later life used a new medium, oil paint on canvas.

Above: Uccello's Battle of San Romano, *painted in about 1450, depicts a minor victory of Florence over Siena in 1432. This panel is in the National Gallery in London.*

Andrea Mantegna

Although originally from Padua, Andrea Mantegna (1431–1506) spent most of his working life in Mantua, where, from 1460, he was court painter to Duke Ludovico Gonzaga, one of the great Renaissance rulers and patrons of the arts. There he spent much of his time decorating the palace. His most famous work is a series of frescoes (1465–74) in the Camera degli Sposi (Wedding Chamber), featuring Duke Ludovico, his family, and his court. Mantegna was a master of perspective and foreshortening—the technique of painting figures and objects convincingly when seen from an unusual angle, such as from below. He incorporated painted, trompe l'oeil architecture into his work, the first artist to do so since ancient times.

Above: In the Camera degli Sposi in Mantua, Mantegna created the illusion of an oculus—a hole in the ceiling open to the sky, with cherubs and court ladies peering down at the viewer. The cherubs in particular show Mantegna's skill in foreshortening.

Fra Angelico

Between 1440 and their unveiling on January 6, 1443, Fra Angelico and a handful of assistants painted nearly 50 frescoes in the Dominican Convent of San Marco. The reconstruction of the convent, which included a library designed by Michelozzo (see page 42), was entirely paid for by Cosimo de' Medici. The *Annunciation* fresco at the head of the stairs is one of the world's most beloved paintings. Mary's eyes are filled with wisdom and humility as she receives Gabriel's momentous message. The enclosed garden outside her loggia is symbolic of Paradise.

Right: In Fra Angelico's Annunciation, *Mary, the protectress of the Dominican friars, is framed by columns with capitals in the style of Michelozzo.*

SHOWCASE: BOTTICELLI, *LA PRIMAVERA*

At the height of his career, Sandro Botticelli (1445–1510) was one of the most successful painters in Florence. He is celebrated above all for two paintings depicting scenes from Roman myth: *La Primavera* (*Spring*, c. 1478), and the *Birth of Venus* (c. 1483). Both were probably commissioned to decorate the palace of Lorenzo di Pierfrancesco de' Medici, a cousin of the great ruler of Florence, Lorenzo de' Medici (Lorenzo the Magnificent, ruled 1469–92). Romantic, poetic, and with no obvious Christian message, they are quite unlike any previous paintings. Botticelli provides an enchanting vision of the mysteries contemplated by the philosophers at Lorenzo's court, and on a large scale: *La Primavera* is over 10 feet (3 m) wide.

La Primavera *depicts the Garden of Venus, the Roman goddess of love, where it is always springtime. The main themes are love, marriage, and fertility.*

The flowers and trees are painted with the kind of meticulous attention to detail seen in paintings of the International Gothic style.

Venus, goddess of love, directs the procession as earthly love is transformed into a higher, spiritual love.

Cupid, Venus's son, is a babylike cherub derived from ancient art. Armed with bow and arrow, he takes aim at the lovestruck.

The three right-hand figures tell the story of Zephyrus the west wind, who falls in love with the nymph Chloris, and, after their marriage, turns her into Flora, goddess of fertility and flowers.

Chloris has now become Flora. Her name had a special resonance in Florence, a city whose name was associated with flowers, and which has lillies as an emblem.

The three Graces, who distribute beauty and charm in the world, wear dresses of thin cloth, revealing bodies that would have been considered ideally shaped in Renaissance times.

Mercury, the messenger of the gods, uses his wand to disperse the clouds so the garden is always full of sunshine.

THE WORLD OF BOSCH

Hieronymus Bosch (c. 1450–1516) mainly lived and worked in his native town of 's-Hertogenbosch, also called Den Bosch, near Brabant. As a young man, Bosch joined the Brotherhood of Our Lady, an elite society that meditated on the punishments awaiting sinners. His fantastical paintings of religious or moral subjects are rendered with a meticulous detail that often seems surreal. Thus, the people in a crowd hounding Jesus as he carries the cross look like crazed, blood-thirsty criminals down to their body piercings and their unshaven chins. In a busy triptych (three-panel painting), the hermit St. Anthony is beset by witches and grotesque, hybrid monsters in a war-ravaged landscape. No more than 25 paintings by Bosch are known. Philip II (1527–98), the devout king of Spain, acquired several of his works, including *The Garden of Earthly Delights*.

Flemish Art

The cities of what is now Belgium (such as Bruges, Ghent, and Brussels) went through a period of great prosperity when they were ruled by the dukes of Burgundy (1384–1482). A number of exceptionally talented artists emerged during this period, producing oil paintings of stunning, luminous detail. They include Jan van Eyck (c. 1390–1441), Rogier van der Weyden (c. 1400–64), and the German-born Hans Memling (c. 1433–94). Their work provides a vivid snapshot of the luxuries (and hardships) of life in the Low Countries at this time.

Below: The triptych of The Garden of Earthly Delights *(c. 1505) is one of the strangest products of Bosch's imagination. It shows the downward trend from the Garden of Eden (left) to the sin and corruption of the world before the Flood (center), and the ghastly, upside-down world of torture and mayhem in hell (right).*

Early Renaissance
North of the Alps

In northern Europe, the Renaissance was deeply influenced by the continuing tradition of Gothic naturalism. Northern artists and humanists were well aware of Renaissance advances in perspective and classical scholarship, even journeying to Italy to increase their knowledge. Yet the Northern Renaissance never entirely fell under the spell of antiquity—Jan van Eyck depicted Adam and Eve as real people instead of statues. Artists exploited a major innovation: oil paint, which was colorful, durable, and capable of fine detail.

Below: Rogier van der Weyden's Descent from the Cross *(c. 1435) is celebrated for its forceful emotions within a highly structured composition.*

SHOWCASE: JAN VAN EYCK, *PORTRAIT OF GIOVANNI ARNOLFINI AND HIS WIFE*

Jan van Eyck was a pioneer of the new technique of oil painting, which he used to create pictures of stunning clarity and brilliantly observed detail. He painted powerful religious works, such as his masterpiece *The Adoration of the Mystic Lamb* (1432), a polyptych (multi-paneled) altarpiece in Ghent Cathedral. This double portrait, dating to 1434, depicts Giovanni Arnolfini, a wealthy Italian banker, and his wife in their home in Bruges. The meaning of the painting is a mystery: It is full of symbols about marriage, fertility, and childbirth, and may have been commissioned to celebrate their marriage, or possibly the death of the wife in childbirth.

The window has been painted with perfect perspective.

Van Eyck's attention to detail is evident everywhere, such as in the light falling on the brass chandelier.

The artist has signed the painting above the mirror with the Latin inscription "Jan van Eyck was here," as if witnessing the marriage.

The convex mirror contains an image of the scene in reverse, including the artist. Relief carvings on the mirror frame depict ten scenes from the story of the death of Christ.

The woman may well be pregnant beneath her robe of bright green, a color symbolizing love and fertility.

The dog is a symbol of faithfulness.

Below: Group of Apostles, *by Veit Stoss, is typical of his style of emotionally charged composition, expression, and gesture.*

The Early Renaissance in France

Trade routes spread right across Europe, and northern European artists followed them to Italy, returning with Renaissance ideas. The leading artist of France of the 15th century, Jean Fouquet (c. 1415–c. 1481) traveled to Italy in about 1443–47; after this his work shows a new approach to perspective, and the influence of classical architecture. Working at the royal court, and appointed royal painter to King Louis XI, Fouquet was celebrated for his portraits. He also produced exquisite illuminated manuscripts, as did his pupil Jean Bourdichon (1457–1521), whose work marks the closing phase of this great medieval art form.

Above: Fouquet's portrait of Guillaume Jouvenel des Ursins reflects the northern European vogue for honest, pious portraiture.

Sculpture

The greatest northern European sculpture of the era was produced for churches. This was a high point of German wood carving, with two outstanding practitioners: Veit Stoss (c. 1450–1533) and Tilman Riemenschneider (c. 1460–1531). Stoss was noted in particular for his realistic depiction of flowing clothing and his exceptionally vivid interpretation of emotion, sometimes underlined by extravagant and exaggerated gestures. Riemenscheider was similarly gifted, but his work tends to be calmer in tone. Many sculptors applied paint to their finished work, but Stoss and Riemenschneider were among the first to leave their finished sculptures unpainted. During this era, altarpieces were often made of painted carvings in high relief, or sometimes as a polyptych combining paintings on the wings with carvings in the central panel. This was a specialty of the Austrian painter and sculptor Michael Pacher (active c. 1465–98). All these sculptors worked in the Renaissance era and were influenced by its trends, but also remained firmly rooted in the traditions of the late Gothic style.

Right: A gilded carving titled The Coronation of the Virgin *forms the central focus of Michael Pacher's altarpiece at the St. Wolfgang Church in Austria.*

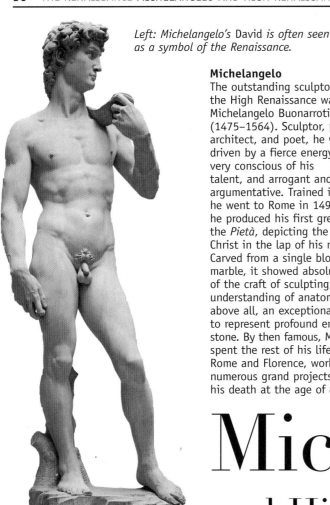

Left: Michelangelo's David is often seen as a symbol of the Renaissance.

Michelangelo

The outstanding sculptor of the High Renaissance was Michelangelo Buonarroti (1475–1564). Sculptor, painter, architect, and poet, he was driven by a fierce energy, very conscious of his talent, and arrogant and argumentative. Trained in Florence, he went to Rome in 1496, where he produced his first great work, the *Pietà*, depicting the dead Christ in the lap of his mother. Carved from a single block of marble, it showed absolute mastery of the craft of sculpting, a deep understanding of anatomy, and, above all, an exceptional ability to represent profound emotion in stone. By then famous, Michelangelo spent the rest of his life between Rome and Florence, working on numerous grand projects until his death at the age of 88.

Above: Michelangelo designed both the architecture and the sculpture for the tomb of Giuliano de' Medici, in the Medici Chapel in Florence (1519–34), but left it unfinished.

Right: The main tools of stone sculpture had changed little for centuries: hammers, big metal chisels for roughing out the stone blocks, fine chisels for the details, and pumice stone for polishing.

Michelangelo
and High Renaissance Sculpture

THE *DAVID*

When Michelangelo returned to Florence in 1501, he was attracted by a challenge set by the Committee of Cathedral Works to make something of a huge block of marble, some 18 feet (5.5 m) long, that an earlier sculptor had abandoned. Michelangelo proposed a statue of David, slayer of Goliath. This was the subject that Donatello had so successfully interpreted in bronze some 60 years earlier (see page 44). But Michelangelo's *David* was going to be different. Instead of triumphantly standing on the head of the defeated Goliath, his *David* is pictured before the battle, sling in one hand, rock in the other, coolly observing his giant enemy. He looks relaxed and confident, mentally and physically steeled for the fight—the perfect image of a Renaissance man, and a symbol for Florence. Michelangelo worked tirelessly on the sculpture for nearly two years. The Committee of Cathedral Works called together 30 leading artists of Florence to decide where this great statue should be placed. Eventually in 1504 it was levered into position outside the Palazzo Vecchio, the town hall of Florence. It stood there until 1873, when it was moved to the Accademia.

By the turn of the century in 1500, the Renaissance had been running for about 150 years. Now a new generation of highly gifted sculptors could build on all the lessons of the past to produce work that truly matched the sculpture of the ancient Greeks. Europe had rulers who wanted to show themselves as great and knowledgeable patrons and were prepared to pay for it. Among them was the new pope, Julius II (reigned 1503–13), who was the patron of many of the best artists of the day, with the result that Rome became the main focus of the High Renaissance. This golden age lasted from about 1500 to 1527, when Rome was sacked and vandalized by troops of Emperor Charles V.

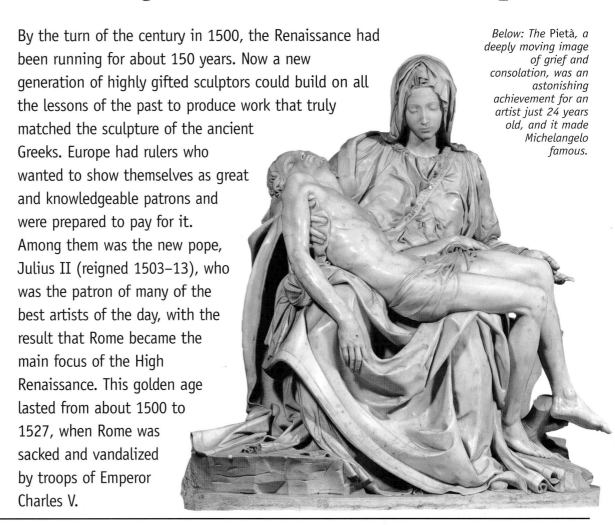

Below: The Pietà, *a deeply moving image of grief and consolation, was an astonishing achievement for an artist just 24 years old, and it made Michelangelo famous.*

SHOWCASE: MICHELANGELO, *MOSES*

In 1505, following his triumph with the *David*, Michelangelo was invited back to Rome by Pope Julius II. This new and ambitious pope had grand plans for Rome, including the complete rebuilding of the Basilica of St. Peter in the Vatican. As part of this plan, Julius II wanted to include a huge tomb for himself. Michelangelo saw this as an opportunity to create his masterpiece, and planned an ornate composition of 40 sculpted figures. The project proved immensely frustrating: Michelangelo spent some 40 years on it, until 1545 (32 years after Julius's death). Only a small part of the original plan was completed, and the tomb was erected in a minor church, St. Peter in Chains, without Julius II in it. After this, Michelangelo devoted his life to architecture, continuing the work at the Basilica of St. Peter.

Moses is depicted with horns in his head, a tradition based on a mistranslation of the Bible, which tells of rays of light coming from Moses's head (rather like a halo).

Moses holds a tablet of stone bearing the Ten Commandments under his right arm.

Moses's muscular bare leg and arms imply tremendous physical strength with which to apply God's law to the world.

The raised robe shows Michelangelo's mastery of depicting cloth.

Moses's seated position might have been more impressive if placed on an upper level and seen from below, as originally planned.

Above: A line drawing of the tomb shows biblical figures on two levels, with Moses in the center at ground level, between statues of Rachel and Leah, Michelangelo's last completed sculptures. His students carved the other figures. The larger-than-life statue of Moses, sculpted by Michelangelo in 1513–15, following Julius II's death, was originally planned as one of four, placed on each corner of a massive rectangular tomb structure.

Benvenuto Cellini

An outstanding sculptor and goldsmith from Florence, Benvenuto Cellini (1500–71) worked in various cities of Italy, accumulating numerous rich and influential patrons, including King Francis I of France and Cosimo de' Medici, Duke of Florence. His most famous work is his exquisite *Saliera* (Salt Cellar), made for Francis I in gold and enamel; but he also made large sculptures, such as his bronze *Perseus Holding the Head of Medusa*.

Like that of Giambologna, his later work has the highly charged drama associated with mannerism. Despite his delicate sensitivities as an artist, Cellini was wild, arrogant, and violent, a crook and a murderer, and often on the run. He wrote a racy and riveting autobiography, which paints a vivid picture of the heady mixture of energy, artistic sophistication, crudeness, and violence of late Renaissance Italy.

Left: Cellini's celebrated Saliera *(1540–43) depicts Neptune, god of the sea, and Ceres, goddess of the Earth, with feet entwined, symbolizing the god-given sources of all food.*

Giambologna

The heir to Michelangelo's reputation as the greatest sculptor of his age was Giambologna (1529–1607), also known as Giovanni da Bologna or Jean de Boulogne: Although working in Italy from 1550, he was in fact born in Douai, France, and trained in Antwerp. He is celebrated for the easy elegance of his work, coupled with powerful, expressive compositions of twisting bodies—a style heavily influenced by Michelangelo and known as mannerism. He worked in Florence, carrying out commissions for the Medici family, and produced large and small sculpture in stone and bronze, as well as elaborate fountains.

Left: Much of Giambologna's work features subjects from classical myth, such as this bronze Flying Mercury (1580), the messenger of the gods.

High Renaissance
Painting in Italy

As with sculpture, painting also reached a new level of sophistication during the High Renaissance in Italy. Techniques in perspective and shading were perfected, making the illusion of three-dimensional space even more convincing. The adoption of oil painting, learned from northern European painters, gave artists the means to shade and model their figures more subtly, and with more intense shadow and vibrant color. In addition, encouraged by their wealthy and powerful patrons, artists took on ever grander subjects, and with ever greater ambition.

Right: In Bacchus and Ariadne (1523–25) Titian illustrated the moment when the riotous god of wine was struck with love at first sight of Ariadne, daughter of King Minos of Crete.

Leonardo da Vinci

A painter, sculptor, engineer, scientist, inventor, and musician, Leonardo da Vinci (1452–1519) was the definitive Renaissance man. Irrepressibly curious about the world around him, Leonardo filled large notebooks with sketches and studies, writing in mirror-image to preserve their secrets. Like Michelangelo after him, he left several works unfinished because they could not capture the beauty of his ideas. In his oil painting, he introduced a subtle shading technique called sfumato to suggest atmosphere, as well as aerial perspective, which gives a sense of depth in landscapes.

Left: Leonardo's Mona Lisa *is the most famous portrait, and the most famous smile, in Western art.*

Below: The invisible spark of life is the central focus of Michelangelo's Creation of Adam *(Sistine Chapel).*

Titian

In Venice a particularly strong tradition of painting emerged in the 16th century, following in the footsteps of Giovanni Bellini (c. 1430–1516). His pupil Tiziano Vecellio, known as Titian (c. 1487–1576), was the leading Venetian painter of the 16th century, and at the time was ranked as highly as Michelangelo. In 1516 he was made the official painter to the Venetian Republic. Titian was renowned for his strong portraits, which seem also to convey a penetrating analysis of character. He also painted religious works and numerous scenes from classical myth, filled with drama and movement, and rich color. Many of these were painted for King Philip II of Spain, one of Titian's main patrons. He also worked for the Gonzaga dukes of Mantua, Emperor Charles V, and Pope Paul III. He died when he was nearly 90 years old.

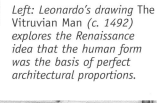

Left: Leonardo's drawing The Vitruvian Man *(c. 1492) explores the Renaissance idea that the human form was the basis of perfect architectural proportions.*

Michelangelo the Painter

Although he considered himself primarily a sculptor, Michelangelo originally trained as a fresco painter. In 1508 Pope Julius II ordered him to put aside his tomb project (see page 51) to take on the immense task of frescoing the ceiling of the Sistine Chapel in the Vatican. After sending away his assistants, Michelangelo worked alone for more than four years (1508–12), painting nearly 300 figures in a complex program of Old Testament scenes separated by prophets, sybils, and the mysterious figures known as *ignudi*. The result was one of the most celebrated triumphs of the Renaissance. Michelangelo painted much as he sculpted, isolating muscular bodies in dramatic poses, emphasized by lighting and shading. Among the first artists to respond to this monumentality was Raphael.

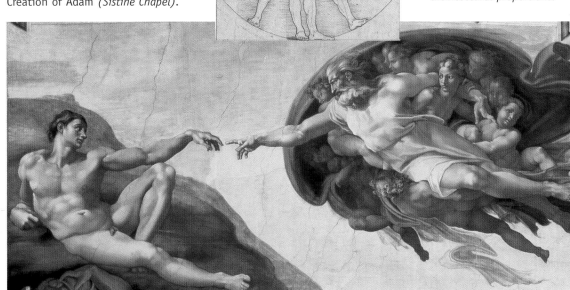

SHOWCASE: RAPHAEL, *THE SCHOOL OF ATHENS*

While Michelangelo was painting the Sistine Chapel ceiling, another of the greatest artists of the era was at work nearby in the Vatican library, painting frescoes in a very different style on the four walls of the Stanza della Segnatura. This was Raffaello Sanzio, known as Raphael (1483–1520), from the city of Urbino. *The School of Athens* occupies one wall: By depicting the heroes of ancient Greek philosophy in the residence of the pope, Raphael was underlining the link between classical wisdom and Christianity.

The architecture resembles the grand classical design that Donato Bramante (1444–1514) had planned for the new Basilica of St. Peter, then under construction.

Euclid (or Archimedes) is bending over to give a lesson in geometry: This is believed to be a portrait of the architect Bramante.

The philosopher Heraclitus, the man leaning on the block of stone, is a portrait of Michelangelo.

Some of the philosophers are actually portraits of leading artists of Raphael's era. Plato is possibly a portrait of Leonardo da Vinci.

Plato and Aristotle take center stage; they were considered by Renaissance scholars to be the greatest of the Greek philosophers.

Raphael has included a portrait of himself, beside the pillar, second from the right.

Giorgione

Giorgio da Castelfranco, known as Giorgione (c. 1477–1510) was another great Venetian painter; he worked alongside Titian on a number of projects, but an early death, at the age of just 33, cut short his career. There is a strange mystery to Giorgione's best-known paintings: The subjects are only vaguely understood, the figures are strangely silent and uncommunicative, and the overall atmosphere is dreamlike. Yet they are painted with superb technique and carefully observed detail. Giorgione was celebrated for his beautiful landscapes, but these are backgrounds to the events portrayed: Pure landscape painting had not yet arrived.

Left: What exactly was Giorgione depicting in The Tempest? *A woman is breast-feeding her child in the open air as a storm approaches. A man stands nonchalantly close by. Does this depict a biblical scene, or is it a painting about fertility, love, and death? Many theories have been suggested to explain the mystery.*

Correggio

Antonio Allegri da Correggio (c. 1489/94–1534) was the leading painter of the city of Parma in northern Italy. His paintings are beautifully modeled, soft, sensuous, and unusually filled with movement. The touching sentiments of Correggio's paintings owe much to the religious paintings of Leonardo da Vinci and Raphael. Correggio was also known for his elaborate ceiling paintings in churches, where he introduced an unprecedented illusion of the dome opening up to reveal the heights of heaven. Correggio's dynamic style was influential on the baroque artists of the 17th century. His subjects included scenes from both the Bible and classical mythology.

Right: Correggio's Nativity Scene *displays his skill at making the angels appear at a height and viewed from below. The golden light coming from the baby Jesus unifies the picture, leading us to the shepherds on the left, then up to the angels, then down again to Mary and the baby Jesus.*

ENGRAVING AND ETCHING

Book printing, which developed after about 1440, had a huge impact on the spread of ideas in the Renaissance. Many printed books were illustrated with pictures. These were usually made from engravings. The engraver drew on a metal plate by cutting lines into it with a sharp instrument; ink would settle in the lines so the picture could be printed. Artists also made prints of their work, to be sold as separate pictures. Another engraving technique was called etching. The metal plate was covered in hard wax, and the artist drew in the wax, scraping down to the metal. The plate was then put in a bath of acid, which "ate" (etched) into any exposed metal, where the artist had drawn. This produced a more subtle and delicate kind of print.

Left: Dürer's precise style of drawing, as seen in this watercolor study of weeds (1503), lent itself to engraving.

Right: A print of The Knight, Death, and the Devil *(1513) shows Dürer's exceptional skill as an engraver.*

High Renaissance
Painting in the North

The impact of the Italian Renaissance was a point of reference for northern artists, who each responded in different ways. Three of Germany's greatest artists lived and worked during the early 16th century: Albrecht Dürer, Matthias Grünewald, and Hans Holbein the Younger. Dürer was the most universal talent, excelling as a painter, draftsman, scientist, and arguably the best engraver of all time. Dürer traveled twice to Venice, taking the time to sketch landscapes along the way. In Italy, he simplified his compositions under the influence of Giovanni Bellini and Mantegna. After 1510, Dürer concentrated his energy and imagination on printmaking, for which he was famous. The backdrop to artistic developments was the growing crisis in religion. Martin Luther led the Protestant revolt. By the second half of the 16th century, Europe was engulfed in turmoil.

Dürer

One of the northern European artists who traveled to Italy was the German painter and printmaker Albrecht Dürer (1471–1528). Born in Nuremberg, he was the son of a goldsmith, who taught him engraving (a skill also used in metalwork) at an early age. Dürer later ran a highly successful printmaking workshop, producing copies of his engravings and etchings. These have an intensity, liveliness, and mastery in drawing that has rarely been matched. Dürer was equally skilled in painting, producing religious works and portraits. He was fascinated by nature and made numerous detailed sketches of plants and animals. He was one of the first artists to produce pure landscape paintings, although only as watercolor sketches.

Right: Dürer painted a number of self-portraits, including this curiously Christ-like one, titled Self-Portrait at the Age of Twenty-eight *(1500).*

SHOWCASE: HANS HOLBEIN, *THE AMBASSADORS*

Hans Holbein the Younger (c. 1497–1543) was the German-born son of a painter. He lived in Switzerland, painting religious subjects until forced to leave by the violent rise of Protestantism. He ended up in England, where his skills in portrait painting were much appreciated by the court of Henry VIII. His many portraits have a distinctive precision, clarity, and honesty to them, offering a fascinating insight into the characters at the center of English life. His large double portrait called *The Ambassadors* was painted in 1553, in oil and tempera on a wooden panel. It depicts the French ambassador to England, Jean de Dinteville, and his friend the Bishop of Lavaur.

Left: With this seal Martin Luther stamped not only documents, but also the tail end of the Renaissance in northern Europe as it entered the new and turbulent era of the Reformation.

Lucas Cranach

The German painter Lucas Cranach the Elder (1472–1553) embodied many of the traditions of northern European early Renaissance painting, with his close attention to detail and polished finish, seen for example in his portraits. But he was a man of his time in other ways. He was a Protestant working in Wittenberg, where in 1517 Martin Luther published his challenge to the church that triggered the Reformation; Cranach painted several portraits of Luther. He was also famous for his small female nudes. In Renaissance fashion, they recall the female nudes of ancient Greek and Roman sculpture, but their naive charm is thoroughly northern European.

Holbein was a master of detail, as seen in his exceptional skill in depicting fur.

The table is laden with scientific and musical instruments and books, indicating that these are Renaissance men: knowledgeable scholars, curious about the world around them but also possessing the sensitivity of musicians.

The mysterious baguette shape in the foreground is in fact a human skull. A visual trick, it only makes sense when viewed from an angle from below. It serves as a symbol of the fragility of life and worldly ambition.

Above: Cranach's popular female nudes, such as Venus and Cupid (1509), were presented as interpretations of classical myth.

Grünewald

Northern European painting always had two contrasting voices: the tranquil precision of Jan van Eyck versus the tense, emotional drama of Rogier van der Weyden (see pages 48–49). The German painter Matthias Grünewald (c. 1480–1528) took the expression of anguish to a new level of intensity. A follower of Martin Luther, he was intensely religious. His most famous work is the Isenheim Altarpiece (c. 1510–15), made for the hospital chapel of the monastery of St. Anthony at Isenheim, on the border between France and Germany. The central panel is a Nativity scene, but on the outside of the wings, which fold over this, is a gruesome, distorted crucifixion, showing a tortured Christ nailed to the cross.

Left: Even the Nativity scene of Grünewald's Isenheim Altarpiece has a passionate intensity.

Above: In Supper at Emmaus *(1601), Caravaggio surprisingly followed Michelangelo's example of showing the resurrected Christ as a young, beardless man.*

Caravaggio

Michelangelo Merisi was born in 1571 in Milan. At age 21 he made his way to Rome. He quickly attracted attention by painting the fortune-tellers and card-players that he saw in the backstreets of the city. His skill at painting still lifes brought him work in a leading studio. Around 1596, his talent was recognized by Cardinal Francesco Maria del Monte, leader of the Medici faction in Rome. The cardinal introduced Caravaggio to other collectors who appreciated his realism. At the turn of the century, Caravaggio's public career was launched in the Contarelli Chapel in San Luigi dei Francesi. Numerous church commissions followed. His successes over the next years overlapped with instances of violence, for which he was arrested. In 1606 Caravaggio murdered a rival in a brawl and was forced to flee Rome. He spent his last years as a fugitive, traveling to Naples, Malta, and Sicily, executing masterpieces in each place.

Caravaggio
and the Art of Reality

During the 1590s in Rome, a young Italian artist called Caravaggio (1571–1610) began a one-man revolution in painting that corresponded to the contemporary advances in science and in literature. At the end of a century torn apart by disputes over religion, Caravaggio and other leading thinkers like Galileo and Shakespeare placed their trust in their own observations. He developed a sensational oil-painting technique, with an attention to light and shadow that we, today, might call photographic. He specialized in dark pictures in which the figures emerge, picked out by a single focused beam of light. It was an extreme form of chiaroscuro (Italian for "light-dark"), a technique of strong shading recommended by Leonardo da Vinci. In addition, Caravaggio painted his friends and neighbors as models for saints and martyrs. The effect was brutally powerful and inevitably controversial.

Georges de La Tour

The French artist Georges de La Tour (1593–1652) came from Lorraine, in eastern France. It is not clear whether he went to Italy, but his style changed radically after 1640, when it begins to show the clear influence of Caravaggio. He used a strong chiaroscuro in religious scenes, and in pictures of social gatherings around card and dice games. He was particularly skilled at showing the effects of candlelight in nighttime scenes, and—as seen in *St. Joseph and Jesus in the Carpenter's Shop* (c. 1640)—delicately reproduced the way that candlelight shines through fingers. His colors are often limited (he loved red), and his faces are often soft and bland, but he could also portray ordinary people with penetrating detail, and sympathy.

Above: Georges de La Tour uses only candlelight to illuminate St. Joseph and Jesus in the Carpenter's Shop. *The figures stand out against a plain background that is nearly black.*

Above: In The Duet *(1628), painted near the end of his short life, Hendrick Ter Brugghen demonstrates how Caravaggio's style could also be applied to cheerful subjects.*

Hendrick Ter Brugghen

"Caravaggism" was particularly popular in the Netherlands, largely as the result of the work of two painters from Utrecht, Hendrick Ter Brugghen (1588–1629) and Gerrit van Honthorst (see page 57). Ter Brugghen spent 10 years in Italy, from 1604 to 1614, where he saw the work of Caravaggio firsthand.

He is well known for his more lighthearted paintings depicting musicians. He was a meticulous observer of detail: His faces often show the imperfections of real life. Although he used the effect of chiaroscuro, in later work his backgrounds tended to be lighter and the overall effect was softer and less brutal than Caravaggio's.

Artemisia Gentileschi

There were very few professional women artists prior to the 20th century. Artemisia Gentileschi (1593–c. 1651) was a notable exception. She was the daughter of Orazio Gentileschi (1563–1639), a respected Caravaggist artist who in 1626 became court painter to King Charles I of England. Artemisia worked in Florence, Rome, Venice, Naples, and London, pursuing a successful career as an artist and an independent woman, a rarity for the times on both counts. She is famous for her very forceful portrayal of women often taking part in dramatic and violent religious scenes—said to be a response to her own personal experience of assault and abuse at the age of 19. For example, she produced a number of paintings on the biblical story of Judith, who seduced and then beheaded the Babylonian general Holofernes in order to save her city from attack.

Left: Gerrit van Honthorst followed Correggio's lead (see page 53) in lighting his Adoration of the Shepherds *(1617) from the Christ child.*

Above right: Judith and Her Maid *(c. 1614), by Artemisia Gentileschi, depicts a determined Judith, armed with the sword that she has used to hack off the head of Holofernes (in the maid's basket).*

Gerrit van Honthorst

Along with his fellow Dutchman Hendrick Ter Brugghen, Gerrit (or Gerard) van Honthorst (1590–1656) spent 10 years of his early career in Rome, from 1610. His paintings at the time were so dark with Caravaggio-style chiaroscuro that he earned the nickname Gerard of the Night. Back in the Netherlands after 1620, he became a leading figure of the Utrecht school and accumulated a wide range of influential patrons. He painted portraits of many members of European royal families and nobility, and from 1637 to 1652 he held the post of official painter to the Dutch court in the Hague. Honthorst's religious scenes have the candlelit intensity of the best Caravaggist work, while his strong chiaroscuro gives a stately elegance to his portraits and society scenes.

SHOWCASE: CARAVAGGIO, *THE CALLING OF ST. MATTHEW*

In July of 1599, Caravaggio received a commission to paint two paintings for the side walls of the Contarelli Chapel in the Church of San Luigi dei Francesi in Rome. They were *The Calling of St. Matthew* and *The Martydom of St. Matthew*. Both works were in place by September 1602 and caused an immediate sensation. *The Calling of St. Matthew* depicts the moment that Levi, a wealthy tax collector, is called by Jesus to be his disciple with the name of Matthew. Caravaggio portrayed Matthew and his companions as if they were gamblers counting their money in a Roman alley. The raking light captures the surprise and confusion of this life-changing moment.

Caravaggio discovered that realism does not rule out spirituality. The strongly raking light also symbolizes the illumination of Matthew's soul.

Jesus looks fixedly at St. Matthew and points at him with the same gesture, in mirror image, with which Adam receives the spark of life on Michelangelo's Sistine Chapel ceiling (see page 52).

St. Matthew cannot believe that Jesus has selected him. By including this unusual gesture, Caravaggio addresses the mystery of grace.

The old man and the stylishly dressed young men are far more interested in the coins on the table.

St. Peter, symbol of the Church, echoes Jesus's gesture. X-rays of these two figures reveal that Caravaggio's first idea was to paint Jesus without a companion.

Above: A busy scene taken from Greek mythology forms part of a ceiling fresco (1684–86) by Luca Giordano in the Palazzo Medici Riccardi.

Luca Giordano
One of the most talented decorative artists working in Italy in the 17th century was Luca Giordano (1632–1705), from Naples. A specialist particularly in ceilings in churches and in palaces, he worked with a natural confidence, and a rapidity that earned him the nickname "Luca Fa Presto" (Luca Does It Quickly). Like all fresco artists, he had to travel to his place of work, which took him to Florence and Venice, and to Madrid, where he spent ten years (1692–1702) in the service of King Charles II of Spain. Influenced by Veronese, whose work he saw in Venice, his compositions are energetic and theatrical, radiant with color, and full of light and air.

Grand Decorations

Above right: The Landing of Marie de' Medici at Marseilles *(1621) formed part of Rubens's series of 24 paintings commissioned by Marie de' Medici for the Palais de Luxembourg in Paris.*

The decoration of churches and palaces achieved a new level of spectacular grandeur in the 17th century. Complex scenes from classical myth and the Bible covered walls and ceilings. The best artists showed an astonishing confidence and verve on a large scale, continuing the tradition of the most talented decorative painters, such as Paolo Veronese (c. 1528–88), working in Venice, and Annibale Carracci (1560–1609), from Bologna. These developments took place against the backdrop of the Counter-Reformation, when the Roman Catholic Church fought back against the tide of Protestantism. In the 17th century, the church found an artistic voice to express its reforming spirit and its new confidence: the lavish and ornate Baroque style (see also pages 68–71).

Peter Paul Rubens
The greatest northern European artist of the Baroque era was Peter Paul Rubens (1577–1640). Following training in Rome, he returned to his hometown of Antwerp in 1608 and rapidly established his reputation as a painter of powerful religious and mythological scenes. Rubens is particularly noted for his dynamic compositions, drawing the eye naturally around sumptuous and highly energized scenes packed with displays of his virtuoso painting skills. Rubens ran a very busy workshop and used assistants and specialist artists to help him with his enormous output. He traveled widely to the courts of Europe, also serving the role of diplomat.

Guido Reni
A leading painter of Bologna, in his day Guido Reni (1575–1642) was considered an artistic genius second only to Raphael, who was his primary inspiration. Reni was noted for his restraint and personal elegance, and these characteristics can be detected in his paintings, even though they often depict highly dramatic and emotional scenes. He produced many individual paintings that were not part of any decorative scheme, but his most celebrated work is *Aurora* (1613–14), a ceiling fresco painted for the powerful Borghese family in Rome.

Below: Guido Reni's Aurora *depicts the god Apollo in his chariot following the figure of Aurora (Dawn), who brings daylight to the world.*

SHOWCASE: ANDREA POZZO,
THE ENTRY OF ST. IGNATIUS INTO HEAVEN

The Italian painter and architect Andrea Pozzo (1642–1709) is celebrated for his extraordinary feats of illusionistic painting, combining painted architecture and the skilled use of foreshortening to stupendous effect. The best example is found at the Church of Sant' Ignazio (St. Ignatius), Rome, where the ceiling has been made to look like a towering extension of the church, reaching up through dramatic classical architecture toward the open heavens above. St. Ignatius of Loyola (1491–1556) was the Spanish founder of the Jesuits, a religious movement that was a potent force in the Counter-Reformation. Pozzo himself was a lay brother of the Jesuit order.

The four continents are represented by women. Clockwise, from top left: Europe, America, Africa, and Asia.

The painting gives the impression that the ceiling has been lifted off the church. All the architecture is painted entirely on a flat surface.

TRICKING THE EYE

Andrea Pozzo was a master of illusion: He could make architecture painted on a flat surface look convincingly three-dimensional. This skilled technique is often referred to as trompe l'oeil. There is a technical Italian word for this effect when it applies to illusionistic architecture: *quadratura* (literally, "squaring"). Pozzo did all his *quadratura* painting, but many decorative artists employed specialists, called *quadraturisti*, to do it for them. The art of creating the illusion of extended space was popular with the Romans, as seen in Pompeii. It was revived in the Renaissance by artists such as Mantegna (see page 47) but reached new heights in the decorative schemes of the Baroque era.

Right: This interior of a dome, in the Church of the Badia in Arezzo, Italy, is in fact a painting on a flat surface by Pozzo.

Beneath the four continents, heathens writhe and tumble in ignorance of the faith.

As St. Ignatius rises to heaven, Christ sends a ray of light to him, which he deflects to the four continents and to missionaries who will spread the gospel around the world.

Giambattista Tiepolo

The last of the great Venetian decorators was Giambattista Tiepolo (1696–1770). A highly gifted artist who worked swiftly with a light and deft touch, he painted numerous large-scale schemes in Italy, as well as in Germany and Spain. His most celebrated work is the fresco at the New Residenz palace in Würzburg in Germany, painted in 1751–53 for the Prince Bishop of Greiffenclau. Covering 7,287 square feet (677 sq. m), it was the world's largest painting at the time, and is still the largest fresco. The subject is Apollo and the four continents, and it features many of the classical gods, plus figures representing Europe, Africa, Asia, and America, and a host of historical figures—all paying homage to the prince bishop.

Right: A detail of Tiepolo's huge fresco at the Residenz in Würzburg shows an angelic figure trumpeting the fame of the prince bishop.

Above: The subject of Ribera's Duel of Isabella de Carazzi and Diambra de Pottinella *(1636) was a real duel between women, fought over a lover, that had taken place in Naples in 1552.*

Jusepe Ribera

One of the leading Spanish painters in Naples was Jusepe (or José) Ribera (1591–1652). Born in Valencia, he went to Rome at the age of 20, where he earned the nickname Lo Spagnoletto (The Little Spaniard); he moved to Naples in 1616, where Velázquez later visited him. Strongly influenced by Caravaggio, and with a very polished technique, he painted mainly scenes from Christian history, and sometimes from classical myth. Many of these depict suffering, and his pictures of elderly, emaciated saints show a brutal honesty toward the physical deterioration that comes with age. He manages nonetheless to give them dignity. The same applies to his famous painting called *The Beggar Known As the Club-Footed Boy* (1642), a study of a handicapped child that is nonetheless dignified and ennobling. Ribera's colors became somewhat lighter in the 1630s. He was also a talented engraver and etcher.

Francisco de Zurbarán

Among the many artists who worked for King Philip IV was Francisco de Zurbarán (1598–1664), who spent two years in Madrid painting 10 pictures for him on the labors of Hercules. Otherwise Zurbarán remained mainly in Seville, painting religious works commissioned for monasteries, both in Spain and in the Americas. These tended to be pictures of monks or saints deep in prayer or experiencing spiritual enlightenment. Many of them are somber works, painted with the strong chiaroscuro of Caravaggio. They evoke a profound religious faith. This kind of work went out of fashion toward the end of Zurbarán's life, and he died in poverty.

Above: With his St. Serapion *(1628), Zurbarán depicted the martyrdom of this medieval monk. Despite its austerity, the painting evokes the dignity of his sacrifice. The cascading folds of his robe have been called "a symphony in white."*

Religious Painting

Spain was a profoundly religious country and was a strong supporter of the Roman Catholic Church in its (often brutal) fight against Protestantism. In addition, with their new territories abroad, the Spanish felt they had a moral duty to spread Christianity through missionary work. Religious conviction and suffering seemed to go hand in hand. The church in Spain demanded art that expressed this outlook. It had been the main patron of the great Mannerist painter known as El Greco (1541–1614); although born in Crete, he moved to Toledo in Spain in about 1577, where he lived and worked for the rest of his life, painting extraordinary, visionary works. The distorted forms and colors of Mannerism were the first expressions of the Counter-Reformation, but the 17th century called for a more sober, realistic style to convey religious devotion and fervor.

Left: The religious paintings of Alonso Cano (1601–67), such as The Vision of St. John *(1635), show the softer style that supplanted Zurbarán.*

Velázquez

and the Golden Age of Spanish Painting

The 17th century marked a high point for Spanish painting. Virtually all Spanish painters were strongly influenced by Italian art, and several of them spent large parts of their careers in Italy, particularly in Naples, which had come under Spanish rule in 1503. Caravaggio was a major source of inspiration. Spain was one of the leading nations in the Age of Exploration, which had begun in the 15th century. Its vast new territories in the Americas and the Far East had made it wealthy and powerful. By the 17th century, Spain was in decline, but it still had plenty of rich patrons. This included King Philip IV (reigned 1621–65), who appointed as his court painter the greatest Spanish artist of the day, Diego Velázquez (1599–1660).

Depicting Everyday Life

Spanish painters of the 17th century showed a fascination with the world that surrounded them. Velázquez painted royal portraits that were dignified but honest: His subjects look like real people. He sought the same dignity when depicting ordinary working people, as in his painting *The Water Seller of Seville* (1623). Several other artists made a speciality of painting the poor. Bartolomé Murillo (1617–82) painted rather sentimental religious paintings, but he also had a sideline in depictions of poor children, such as *Beggar Boys Eating Grapes* (c. 1650). This concern with portraying the real world extended also to everyday objects. Fruit, vegetables, dishes, and glasses on a table now became the subject of still-life paintings. Juan Sánchez Cotán (1560–1627) was an exceptional still-life painter. When he was about 43 years old, he became a monk, suggesting that he saw God's work in the objects that he so meticulously painted.

Left: Murillo captures a spontaneous moment of pleasure in A Girl and Her Dueña *(governess), painted in 1670.*

Below: Quince, Cabbage, Melon, and Cucumber *is the title of this arresting still life painted by Sánchez Cotán in about 1602. A strong light illuminates the simple objects suspended in a curving shape in front of a mysterious space.*

SHOWCASE: DIEGO VELÁZQUEZ, *LAS MENIÑAS*

Diego Velázquez painted religious and mythological scenes, but he was also celebrated as a portrait painter. The masterpiece of his final years is *Las Meniñas* (1656). The title means "The Maids of Honor," referring to the young women who stand on either side of the blond, five-year-old infanta (princess), Margarita. The painting is a teasing puzzle, playing with role reversal. Velázquez depicts himself on the left, painting at a huge canvas. He is actually painting the king and queen, who can be seen in the mirror at the back. So we, the viewers, are standing in the shoes of royalty. The infanta has simply come to watch, so this is not at all like the usual official portraits; instead, as in a snapshot, it depicts an informal moment in the life of the royal court.

Velázquez wears the Cross of the Order of Santiago, an honor bestowed by the king, underlining the high status now accorded to artists.

A member of the queen's staff stands in the doorway.

The maids of honor hover beside the infanta attentively.

The dwarf court jester pokes the sleepy dog with his foot, adding to the informality of the scene.

The royal court included dwarfs, who provided entertainment. Mari Bárbola acts as a striking contrast to the conventionally pretty infanta.

The detail looks sharp, but in fact Velázquez applied a relatively loose technique using long-handled brushes, knowing that the painting would be seen at a distance.

Domestic Scenes

The Dutch art-buying public—which included people at almost all levels of the social scale—had a particular fondness for paintings that depicted scenes taking place inside the kinds of homes in which they themselves lived. Such pictures were called genre paintings. Some showed scenes of great poise and tranquillity. A great master of this kind of painting was Pieter de Hooch (1629–84). The objects and the people depicted in his work seem to acquire a greater weight and significance simply because de Hooch has done them the honor of painting them. Other artists, such as Jan Steen (c. 1629–79), chose to paint more raucous scenes of family gatherings and parties eating and drinking. Genre paintings are never quite as straightforward as they seem: They are full of symbols—instantly recognizable to viewers in the know—that point to story elements in the scene, such as love, infidelity, greed, or the ever-present threat of death.

Right: In St. Nicholas Day *(c. 1660–65) Jan Steen portrays a family on the day of present-giving, with all the joy, misery, and resentment that it entails.*

Left: Paintings like The Messenger *(c. 1669), by Pieter de Hooch, offer a vivid insight into the lifestyles of 17th-century Holland.*

Vermeer
and Dutch Painters of Everyday Life

The clash between Protestants and the Roman Catholic Church led to the violent partition of the Spanish Netherlands and, in 1581, the creation of the independent, and largely Protestant, United Provinces (today's Netherlands, or Holland). This was a period of rapidly expanding trade and empire building, and very quickly the Netherlands became rich, notably through its possession of the Spice Islands of Indonesia. The early 17th century was known as the Golden Age. The newly wealthy middle classes had a taste for pictures that mirrored their own lives: domestic scenes inside their homes, depictions of daily life, still lifes, views of cities, landscapes, and seascapes. The result was a style of brilliantly crafted, intimate, and beguiling paintings that was utterly Dutch in spirit.

Close Observation

Like the northern European painters of the early Renaissance, Dutch artists could analyze and paint objects in the finest detail. Artists such as Pieter Claesz (1597/8–1661) raised still-life painting to a new level of excellence, able to make ordinary things seem wondrous and precious. In *The Goldfinch* (c. 1654), Carel Fabritius (1622–54) used this same intense observation to charming effect. A pupil of Rembrandt (see pages 64–65), Fabritius was one of the most gifted artists of his generation, but an explosion in a gunpowder store in Delft cut short his life and destroyed most of his work.

Above: Fabritius's Goldfinch *is a small painting, about the size of this book, and has the intimate appeal and captivating detail that is typical of Dutch painting.*

Above: Adriaen Brouwer (1605/6–38) is famous for his often witty lowlife scenes of excess in taverns. In The Bitter Tonic *(c. 1635) he pokes fun at the discomfort of the drinker.*

Dutch Landscapes

Dutch artists were among the first to create pure landscape paintings: straightforward observations of the scene, not as a background to figures telling a story. They painted the Netherlands—its towns, its countryside, its ships in harbors and at sea—all with the same atmospheric detail that the genre painters used. By depicting and celebrating all aspects of the landscape of the newly independent Netherlands, these paintings also appealed to the patriotic instincts of Dutch buyers. An early pioneer was Jan van Goyen (1596–1656), who captured the moody beauty of Holland's watery landscape. Other specialists included Aelbert Cuyp (1620–91), Jacob van Ruisdael (1628–82), and Meindert Hobbema (1638–1709). Landscape artists made sketches outdoors, but the finished oil paintings were done in the studio—and very often were only approximate depictions of a particular location.

Above: Vermeer gave a rare demonstration of his talent for landscape in his View of Delft from the Rotterdam Canal *(c. 1660).*

SHOWCASE: JAN VERMEER, *THE MILKMAID*

Left: A detail from The Milkmaid *shows Vermeer's brilliant still-life technique. Tiny raised spots of paint indicate the sparkle of light on the bread and on the rim of the jug.*

The colors have been carefully restricted, mainly to blue and yellow.

The figure of the maid has been boldly sculpted with shading to make her look almost three-dimensional against the flat, white background.

The wooden box is a foot warmer, into which hot coals were placed. It was a symbol of love and courting. The ceramic tile on its left seems to have a picture of Cupid, god of love, with his bow, painted on it.

The greatest of all the Dutch genre painters was Jan Vermeer (1632–75). Not much is known about his life: He lived in Delft and painted painstaking works of immense charm and tranquillity, and with such a sense of atmosphere and moment that you can almost hear them. Only 35 works by Vermeer are known; most are interior scenes. *The Milkmaid* (1658–60) is unusual in that it depicts a maidservant rather than someone more well-to-do, but he treats her with just as much care and attention to detail. Can you hear the sound of the milk being poured?

Left: The Jewish Bride *(c. 1667) is painted with the glowing light and loose brushwork typical of Rembrandt's final decade.*

Right: The Laughing Cavalier *fixes the viewer with a captivating grin. Hals conveys a real character beneath the swagger of his elaborate costume.*

Rembrandt

Rembrandt Harmenszoon van Rijn (1606–69), the son of a miller and a baker's daughter, demonstrated his talent for art at an early age. Working in the Hague, the location of the royal court, he established himself as a successful society portrait artist. In 1631 he moved to Amsterdam, where there was an even bigger and more receptive client base; he worked with a major art dealer, Hendrick Uylenburgh, and married his niece. He also painted religious subjects and produced hundreds of prints. Over time, his portraits became more penetrating, and his technique became looser, more spontaneous. His best portraits of his later years are astonishing, flickering insights into personality. Unfortunately, his clients did not appreciate this shift in style and emphasis, and Rembrandt lost interest in pleasing them. He died almost forgotten, in poverty.

Frans Hals

The wealthy clients of Dutch portrait artists in the 17th century wanted paintings that were true likenesses but showed them in the best light—just as we might choose portrait photographs of our family today. They liked a smooth and polished style that reproduced faithfully not only the face, but also clothing and detail—such as their elaborate white ruffs (collars). An outstanding Dutch portrait artist of the generation before Rembrandt was Frans Hals (c. 1581–1666) of Haarlem. He painted his portraits to suit the subject: sometimes very detailed, precise, and polished (for wealthy clients), sometimes with loose, rapid brushstrokes. Generally, he depicts his sitter in a relaxed and happy frame of mind, and there is no better example of this than his most famous work, *The Laughing Cavalier* (1624).

Rembrandt
and Dutch Portraits
in the Golden Age

The outstanding Dutch artist of the 17th century was Rembrandt. He saw himself as a rival to Rubens, the great Flemish painter from Antwerp who was nearly 30 years his senior. But in fact they were working in quite different circumstances. Rubens was very successful in the Spanish Netherlands, working for the Roman Catholic Church and for the flamboyant royal courts of Europe in the full, grandiose flourish of the Baroque era. The Dutch were Protestant and had a streak of puritanical severity that came from their Calvinist form of Protestantism. Rembrandt's clients wanted pictures that reflected their outlook: pious, public-spirited, hardworking, dignified, honest, and fully aware of human frailty. Perhaps it is not surprising, then, that Dutch painters of this period produced some of the most penetrating portraits ever made.

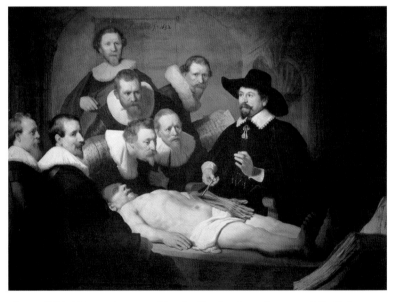

Above: With his novel composition in The Anatomy Lesson of Dr. Tulp *(1632), Rembrandt brought a sense of dynamism to group portraiture.*

Group Portraits

Rembrandt, Hals, and the other portrait artists of the day were often asked to do group portraits. The clients were sometimes individuals who wanted their whole families portrayed in a single painting, or they were institutions of some kind—such as doctors' societies, the governors of a charity, or military clubs—who wanted a record of their members to hang in their offices. With institutions, it was often the case that the people in the portrait shared the cost. The traditional way of painting this kind of group portrait was to depict each individual with equal emphasis, sitting in a row or around a table. But the result was often rather dull. Rembrandt realized that a group portrait could have more spirit and verve with a more varied composition, and with some interaction between the sitters. He broke the mold with his *Anatomy Lesson of Dr. Tulp*, a painting that caused a sensation and made his name when he first arrived in Amsterdam as a young artist.

Above: Using rapid brushwork, Frans Hals captures a playful, spontaneous glance in his Gypsy Girl *(1628-30).*

The Inner Self

It was part of the northern European tradition to pursue honesty in art, and this thread ran through Dutch painting. It can be seen in the work of Frans Hals, particularly in his more informal portraits, such as the *Gypsy Girl*. Rembrandt shows a strong tendency toward introspection in his many self-portraits—a tendency that increased with age. Gradually his image of himself became less self-assured and flamboyant, less concerned about his appearance, but more adept at revealing his inner soul. Rembrandt's pupil, Gerrit Dou (1613–75), painted small, intense pictures of individual people surrounded by fine objects and quietly concentrating on their work.

Above: In A Painter in His Studio *(1647), Gerrit Dou paints himself amid a clutter of items symbolizing his interests, studies, and achievements.*

SHOWCASE: REMBRANDT, *THE NIGHT WATCH*

Rembrandt's most celebrated group portrait is a huge painting known as *The Night Watch*, painted in 1642 when he was at the height of his fame. The original title was *The Young Lord Van Purmerlandt, As Captain, Orders His Lieutenant, the Lord Van Vlaerderdingen, to March His Company Out*. It shows a company of the civic guard—which doubled as a kind of officers' social club—setting out from their headquarters, probably for an official reception rather than to perform the night watch. There were 16 subscribers who paid different fees to be included in the painting, so Rembrandt was able to vary the emphasis on the faces; this allowed greater freedom in the composition. Nonetheless, all the key portraits are clearly visible.

The painting was originally bigger but was trimmed on all sides to fit a space in Amsterdam's town hall when it was moved there in 1715.

This branch of the civic guard were musketeers. Muskets changed the face of warfare in the 17th century, replacing the pike (held by the man in the tall hat to the rear).

The picture focuses on the two main officers, who are painted almost life-size.

Many of the characters are busy doing something, which gives the painting a greater sense of animation than is usual for group portraits.

The only female character serves as a kind of mascot, and carries the company's emblem on her belt: bird's claws.

Rembrandt used a strong chiaroscuro technique in his portraits, but the varnish used to protect this painting went darker with time, making it look even more like a night scene.

Claude Lorrain
In marked contrast to the dynamism and swagger of popular Baroque painters such as Rubens (see page 58), Claude Lorrain (c. 1600–82) painted pictures of deep serenity. The main feature is often a stunningly beautiful, idealized landscape bathed in a soft and dreamy light. Lorrain usually created these landscapes as a background for small groups of figures depicting a story from the Bible or classical myth. But sometimes these are purely landscapes. Imaginary and always carefully composed, they were painted in the studio but based on drawings and painted sketches made outdoors. Lorrain came from a poor family in the area of northeast France called Lorraine, hence his name (his real name was Claude Gellée). He spent most of his working life in and around Rome.

Left: Claude Lorrain painted numerous harbor scenes in his soft and luminous style, such as Harbor with Villa Medici *(1637).*

Jacques Callot
One of the first artists to produce only prints and drawings, Jacques Callot (1592–1635) went to Italy as a youth and worked in Rome and Florence before returning to France in 1621. His prints have the exaggerated distortions of the Italian mannerists and often focus on the grotesque—a popular taste at the time of Louis XIII. His greatest work was a series of shockingly blunt etchings called *The Great Miseries of War*, begun in 1633.

Right: Jacques Callot's etching of a beggar on crutches is typical of his subject matter.

Poussin
and French Artists of the 17th Century

In the 17th century, France was the new rising power of Europe. It had the largest population: 21 million, when Spain had 7 million and the British Isles just 5.5 million. Whereas in the Netherlands considerable wealth was in the hands of the middle classes, in France it was concentrated in the hands of relatively few aristocratic landowners. They lived in large châteaus in the countryside and attended court in Paris. The royal court became ever more powerful, grand, and extravagant, first under King Louis XIII (reigned 1610–43), then under Louis XIV (reigned 1643–1715), who created Europe's most magnificent palace at Versailles (see page 71). The taste in art of the ruling elite reflected its members' wealth, privilege, and sense of grandeur. Most of the leading French artists studied in Rome before returning to Paris to enter the royal art academy founded in 1648.

Above: Landscape dominates Poussin's mournful depiction of a ceremony for an ancient Greek statesman in The Funeral of Phocion *(1648).*

Nicolas Poussin
The influence of classical Rome is particularly apparent in the paintings of Nicolas Poussin (1594–1665). The son of a French farmer from Normandy, he worked in Paris, then went to Rome in 1624, where he stayed for the rest of his career—except for a brief spell in 1640–42 when he was appointed court painter to Louis XIII. He painted scenes from the Bible and mythology, often depicting incidents of high action, but his figures appear almost frozen in motion, like statues. He had a gift for inventing Arcadian landscapes based on geometric forms. His paintings stand out for their sense of calculation and control, even when depicting extremely animated scenes such as battles and bacchanalian revels.

SHOWCASE: POUSSIN, *THE SHEPHERDS OF ARCADIA*

This famous painting of 1638 shows Nicholas Poussin at the height of his powers. The painting has the meditative calm of a pastoral poem. The landscape appears natural, yet it is purified of every accident or blemish. In the midst of their idyllic existence, four ancient wayfarers come across a tomb and read its inscription. They are surprised and moved to read its epitaph, for it is addressed to them: "*Et in Arcadia ego*"("Even in Arcadia, I [Death] am present").

The picturesque, rocky background suggests that the group is surrounded by a Mediterranean landscape of restrained beauty.

The woman's hand on the young man's shoulder is thoughtful and consoling.

Their clothing has been carefully coordinated in the three primary colors: red, yellow, and blue.

The figures are modeled like classical statuary and placed in a row like an ancient bas-relief.

Simon Vouet

In his day, Simon Vouet (1590–1649) was much admired and very successful, and he had a strong influence on the developing tastes of the French court. He worked in Italy from 1613 to 1627, but then returned to Paris to become court painter to Louis XIII (preceding Poussin in that role). Blending the sumptuous, flowing Baroque style with the costumes and poses of classicism, he painted religious and mythological scenes full of movement, vivid primary colors, and billowing robes.

Left: Simon Vouet's Allegory of Wealth *(c. 1630) may have been painted as part of the decorative program of the château of Saint-Germain.*

The Le Nain Brothers

There were three Le Nain brothers: Antoine (c. 1588–1648), Louis (c. 1593–1648), and Mathieu (c. 1607–77). They worked together in Paris and painted in a similar, distinctive style, with strong compositions of figures in contemporary social scenes and biblical scenes, sometimes glamorous, sometimes brutally realistic. Their pictures tend to be sharply lit with Caravaggesque chiaroscuro. They all signed their paintings simply with "Le Nain," so scholars long debated their identities. Louis is admired for his frank and sympathetic paintings of peasants at work and in their homes.

Right: Supper at Emmaus *(1645), attributed to Mathieu Le Nain, takes on the same subject as Caravaggio (see page 56), but with a French accent.*

Bernini
and European Sculpture of the 17th Century

The energy, passion, and swagger of Baroque painting (see pages 58–59) had its equivalent in sculpture. It was a style favored by the Roman Catholic Church, which was intent on putting forward a magnificent face following the crisis of the Reformation. Indeed the perfect expression of the Baroque was an elaborate church design that combined architecture, sculpture, and painting in a triumphant show of curved volutes, stately columns, and rich decoration. The dominant figure of this period was the Italian Gianlorenzo Bernini (1598–1680), who was also a gifted architect and painter.

Right: François Duquesnoy's greatest work is his statue of St. Andrew (1629–33), with his x-shaped cross, for the Basilica of St. Peter, in the Vatican.

Left: Puget's Milo of Croton *(1672–82) depicts the famous ancient Greek wrestling champion being attacked by a lion.*

Gianlorenzo Bernini

Bernini brought a fresh verve to sculpture. His figures are full of movement: With flowing drapery and delicate, outstretched limbs and fingers, they seem to bring marble miraculously to life. Bernini was the son of a sculptor, and he showed early talent. In Rome, his father was able to introduce him to the leading patrons. For Cardinal Scipione Borghese, Bernini produced four large sculptures in 1618–25, which included his *David*. These made his name, and for the rest of his life, Bernini worked mainly for the popes, as both a sculptor and architect (see page 70). There were a number of other very gifted sculptors in Rome at this time, including the Italian Alessandro Algardi (1598–1654), his main rival, and Brussels-born François Duquesnoy (1597–1643). But Bernini outshone them all.

France

The grandiose gesture of the Baroque style appealed to the authorities of both church and state. King Louis XIV of France upheld the divine right of kings—the God-given right to wield absolute power. He summoned Bernini to France in the summer of 1665 in order to complete designs for the Louvre. Bernini's plans were not executed, but during his sojourn he sculpted the king's portrait in marble. Working for Louis XIV at his vast new palace at Versailles (see page 71) were Antoine Coysevox (1640–1720), a sculptor in the Baroque tradition, and François Girardon (1628–1715), a more classical sculptor. Pierre Puget (1620–94) was one of the most gifted Baroque sculptors, but relatively few of his works were accepted at Versailles; his *Milo of Croton* (1672–82) was a rare exception. Perhaps his work was too powerfully emotional, but in any case Puget found the court intrigues intolerable and instead spent most of his working life in the southern port city of Marseilles.

Right: Bernini often sculpted his work so it could be admired from all angles, as seen in his David *(1623), depicted in the moment before his slingshot throw.*

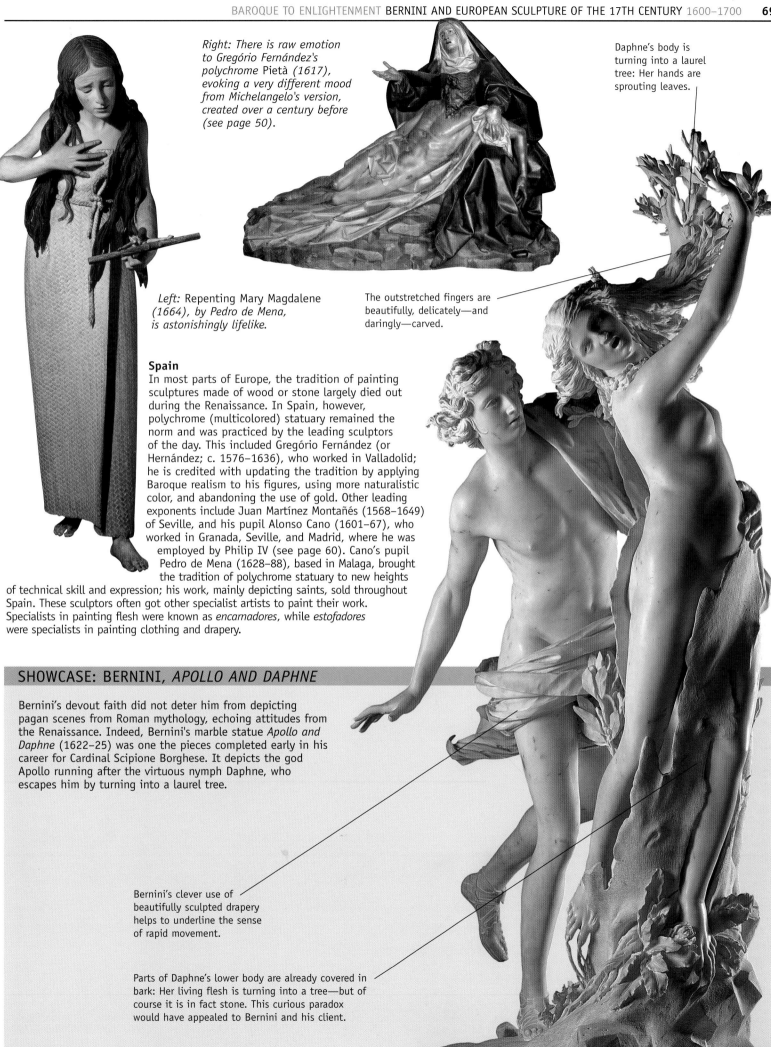

Right: There is raw emotion to Gregório Fernández's polychrome Pietà *(1617), evoking a very different mood from Michelangelo's version, created over a century before (see page 50).*

Daphne's body is turning into a laurel tree: Her hands are sprouting leaves.

Left: Repenting Mary Magdalene *(1664), by Pedro de Mena, is astonishingly lifelike.*

The outstretched fingers are beautifully, delicately—and daringly—carved.

Spain

In most parts of Europe, the tradition of painting sculptures made of wood or stone largely died out during the Renaissance. In Spain, however, polychrome (multicolored) statuary remained the norm and was practiced by the leading sculptors of the day. This included Gregório Fernández (or Hernández; c. 1576–1636), who worked in Valladolid; he is credited with updating the tradition by applying Baroque realism to his figures, using more naturalistic color, and abandoning the use of gold. Other leading exponents include Juan Martínez Montañés (1568–1649) of Seville, and his pupil Alonso Cano (1601–67), who worked in Granada, Seville, and Madrid, where he was employed by Philip IV (see page 60). Cano's pupil Pedro de Mena (1628–88), based in Malaga, brought the tradition of polychrome statuary to new heights of technical skill and expression; his work, mainly depicting saints, sold throughout Spain. These sculptors often got other specialist artists to paint their work. Specialists in painting flesh were known as *encarnadores*, while *estofadores* were specialists in painting clothing and drapery.

SHOWCASE: BERNINI, *APOLLO AND DAPHNE*

Bernini's devout faith did not deter him from depicting pagan scenes from Roman mythology, echoing attitudes from the Renaissance. Indeed, Bernini's marble statue *Apollo and Daphne* (1622–25) was one the pieces completed early in his career for Cardinal Scipione Borghese. It depicts the god Apollo running after the virtuous nymph Daphne, who escapes him by turning into a laurel tree.

Bernini's clever use of beautifully sculpted drapery helps to underline the sense of rapid movement.

Parts of Daphne's lower body are already covered in bark: Her living flesh is turning into a tree—but of course it is in fact stone. This curious paradox would have appealed to Bernini and his client.

Baroque and Rococo
Architecture

The Baroque style was designed to impress. Thus it found favor with the ruling authorities of the 17th century. Baroque architecture takes classical features such as Corinthian columns and capitals, and temple-like pediments, and launches them into movement. Although the floor plans are symmetrical, the building outlines are animated by an unclassical interplay of projection and recession. Curves, swags, and other ornaments dot the surface. The Rococo style took this one stage further: Interiors are a frothy confection of curls and swirls, garlands and cherubs, often gilded against white plaster stucco, and asymmetrical in design. The word *rococo* has a rather obscure origin in the "rocaille" shellwork used to decorate the garden grottoes and fountains of the wealthy. It was often dismissed as lighthearted and frivolous, but the Rococo style could also be deliciously exuberant and uplifting.

Below: The octagonal Church of Santa Maria della Salute (1631–81) in Venice is a Baroque masterpiece by Baldassarre Longhena (1598–1682).

Above: Bernini's oval colonnade in front of the Basilica of St. Peter was built in 1656–67. With space to hold crowds of 300,000, it symbolizes the church's embrace of all the faithful.

Bernini's Architecture

Early in his career, under Pope Urban VIII (reigned 1623–44), Bernini became principal artist to the papal court. He made his name as a designer with his elaborate bronze baldachin (canopy) over the high altar in the Basilica of St. Peter in the Vatican. He fell somewhat out of favor with Pope Innocent X (1644–55) but was restored to prominence by Pope Alexander VII (1655–67). It was then that Bernini carried out his greatest architectural undertaking: the creation of the great oval colonnade around the piazza in front of St Peter's. He also designed the exquisite small baroque Church of Sant'Andrea al Quirinale (1658–78), decorated inside with colored marble and stucco, and lit from the oculus of the oval dome. In addition to churches, Bernini designed a number of palazzi (private mansions) in Rome, including the Palazzo Barberini (with Borromini) and the Palazzo Chigi-Odescalchi.

Borromini

In architecture, Bernini's great rival in Rome was Francesco Borromini (1599–1667). His style of baroque was daring and imaginative: In his churches he created startling confections of circles and triangles, but—in contrast to Bernini—his interiors were relatively simply decorated with white stucco. Borromini was irritable and melancholic, which put clients off; he completed comparatively few projects.

Right: The dome and spiraling steeple of the Church of Sant'Ivo alla Sapienza (1640–50) in Rome are typical of Borromini's innovative approach.

Outside Rome

The Baroque style of architecture was readily adopted not only across Italy, but also across Europe, and the Spanish took it to the Americas to build churches in their new colonies. Born in Brazil, Aleijadinho (1730–1814) was a sculptor and architect of prodigious talent. The style was adopted by Protestant countries as well. In England, for instance, Christopher Wren 1632–1723) rebuilt St. Paul's Cathedral(1675–1708) in Baroque style.

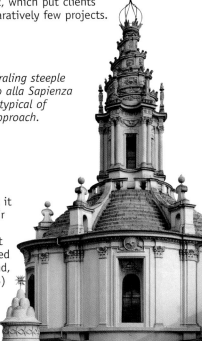

Versailles

The Baroque style was adopted in France by the architects of the new, grand châteaux, starting with Vaux-le-Vicomte (1658–61), designed by Louis Le Vau (1612–70) and Charles Le Brun (1619–90). Le Brun then worked with Jules Hardouin-Mansart (1646–1708) on the greatest royal palace of Europe: Versailles. Louis XIV's vast project began in 1668 and involved some 30,000 laborers. The royal court moved there in 1682. Versailles was not simply a residence for the Sun King and his family. It was a massive public showcase, attended by 7,000 courtiers and a further 14,000 staff and daily visitors. Work continued well into the next century, under Louis XV and Louis XVI.

Rococo Churches

As an architectural style, Rococo (often overlapping with late Baroque) had the most impact in Germany, Austria, and the countries of eastern Europe. Typically, the churches are fronted by pairs of white, tiered towers with onion-shaped domes, while the interiors sparkle with gilded ornament. A number of such churches were built in Catholic Bavaria, including the fabulously ornate basilica for the Benedictine abbey of Ottobeuren, designed by Johann Michael Fischer (1692–1766), and the Wieskirche (1745–54), by Domenikus Zimmermann (1685–1766).

Above: The interior of the Church of St. Nicholas (1732–35) in Prague is the masterpiece of the Czech father-and-son team Christoph (1655–1722) and Kilian Ignaz Dientzenhofer (1689-1751).

Left: Versailles' huge and glittering Hall of Mirrors was designed by Jules Hardouin-Mansart and completed in 1684. It is named after the 17 large mirrors that line one side.

SHOWCASE: PIAZZA NAVONA, ROME

Rome's most beautiful square, Piazza Navona, stands on the site of an oval athletic stadium where the ancient Romans came to watch *agones* (games). Pope Innocent X gave the square a Baroque face-lift. Bernini was commissioned to create public fountains, and Borromini was invited to complete the Church of Sant'Agnese in Agone (1653–57), which had been started by Girolamo Rainaldi (1570–1655).

Borromini's main contribution to the Church of Sant'Agnese in Agone was the facade. The arrangement of the dome and two belfries had a major influence on Baroque style in Europe.

The fountain is the base of an ancient obelisk brought from Egypt.

At the center of the square is the *Fountain of the Four Rivers*, one of Bernini's most famous works, installed in 1651. The main rivers of the four continents are represented symbolically by river gods, animals, and plants.

Next door is the Palazzo Pamphili (1644–50), residence of the family of Pope Innocent X, designed by Girolamo Rainaldi.

18th-Century Sculpture
Rococo to Enlightenment

The lighthearted frivolity of the rococo style suited in particular the French aristocratic life of Versailles, especially under King Louis XV (reigned 1715–74)— wealthy, luxurious, pleasure-seeking, and self-indulgent. In sculpture, the Rococo has all the lightness of Bernini's Baroque, without the serious themes. But by the 1760s there was a new mood afoot. Scholars and writers and many serious-minded people were beginning to study the world and demand answers based on logic and scientific proof. What started off as a new Age of Reason evolved into the Enlightenment. Art, in response to this more serious mood, took a fresh look at classical models.

Left: Messerschmidt named this alabaster character head A Deliberate Buffoon.

Expression
Working in Vienna, the German-born sculptor Franz Xaver Messerschmidt (1736–83) made standard Baroque portrait busts of members of the royal court, and sculptures of religious subjects. But in the 1770s, influenced by early Roman portrait busts, he began a series of "character heads," many of them pulling extreme faces. He made some 70 of these in all. A similar interest in facial expression had interested Leonardo da Vinci, and Messerschmidt's quest echoes an Enlightenment fascination with the workings of the human mind. But in fact Messerschmidt's character heads also coincided with his own increasingly unstable state of mind.

Left: Houdon's full-length portrait of the French writer and philosopher Voltaire (1781) was commissioned by Voltaire's niece after his death.

Jean-Antoine Houdon
Celebrated for his portraits, the French sculptor Jean-Antoine Houdon (1741–1828) knew personally—and portrayed—many of the key figures of the French Enlightenment, including the writers and philosophers Denis Diderot (1771) and Jean-Jacques Rousseau (1778). In 1778–79, he also met and portrayed the American writer, scientist, and politician Benjamin Franklin, and Franklin persuaded him to go to the newly independent United States to portray George Washington (1785–88) and Thomas Jefferson (1789). To all these projects, he brought a fresh style that fit well with the new age: classical in its refinement, Baroque in its grand spirit, but also invigorated by the natural observation of the Enlightenment.

Monumental Sculpture
Echoing the Romans, rulers during the Enlightenment liked to erect public statues to underline their right to rule and ensure their lasting legacies. In 1785–88, Houdon made a full-length standing statue of George Washington for the Virginia state capitol in Richmond. The French sculptor Étienne-Maurice Falconet (1716–91) was known for his Rococo depictions of women and cherubs, but his masterpiece was a bronze statue of Peter the Great of Russia (reigned 1682–1725), erected in St. Petersburg, then the capital of Russia. Completed in 1782, it had been commissioned by Empress Catherine the Great (reigned 1762–96), a notable patron of Enlightenment artists and writers.

Right: Falconet's bronze equestrian statue of Peter the Great, in St. Petersburg, was technically daring, with all the weight taken by the horse's two back legs and the tail.

Rococo Stucco

Stucco is a kind of light plaster made of lime mixed with powdered marble and glue. When it dries it becomes hard and a brilliant white. While damp, it can be shaped and carved into architectural decorations of considerable complexity. By adding extra glue, stucco can also be polished to appear much like marble. As a technique capable of creating a mass of architectural ornament, it suited the Rococo perfectly. One of the greatest *stuccatori* (stucco artists) was the Sicilian Giacomo Serpotta (1656–1732), who worked mainly in churches in Palermo. His most famous decorative schemes are found at the Oratory of San Lorenzo (1690–1706) and the Oratory of the Rosary of San Domenico (1710–17), both in Palermo.

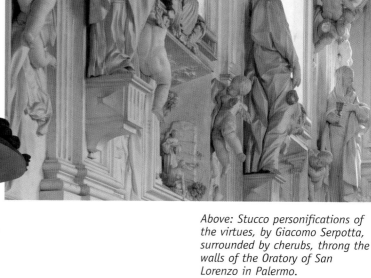

Above: Stucco personifications of the virtues, by Giacomo Serpotta, surrounded by cherubs, throng the walls of the Oratory of San Lorenzo in Palermo.

SHOWCASE: CLODION, *TWO NYMPHS WITH A BOWL OF FRUIT*

Claude Michel, known as Clodion (1738–1814), was a highly successful Rococo sculptor, producing charming, small statuettes, usually on themes drawn from classical myth—dancing and frolicking nymphs, satyrs, and cupids. Born in Nancy, he worked in Paris, and lived in Rome from 1762 to 1771, where he studied classical, Renaissance, and Baroque sculpture. Although he worked in many media, Clodion is best known for his statuettes made of terra-cotta—a medium primarily used by sculptors to make preparatory studies for larger works.

This plaster work, standing nearly 8 feet (2.35 m) high, was built around a wooden and iron framework, which provides stability to the graceful figures. It is dated around 1785.

The use of cloth to indicate movement is reminiscent of Bernini.

Both figures are delicately poised on one foot, enhancing their gracefulness.

Funerary Monuments

The elaborate, otherworldly tone of high Baroque and Rococo sculpture was particularly well-suited to tombs and memorials to the dead. Such monuments are designed to inspire thoughtful meditation on human achievements. A fine example is the tomb of Sir Isaac Newton (1643–1727), the great English scientist, astronomer, and mathematician, in Westminster Abbey in London. It was designed by the English architect William Kent (1685–1748) and made by the Flemish-born sculptor John Michael Rysbrack (1694–1770). Newton is depicted reclining on his books, pointing to a scroll bearing mathematical designs, held by two cherubs. Above him, a personification of astronomy lies on top of the globe, resting on a book.

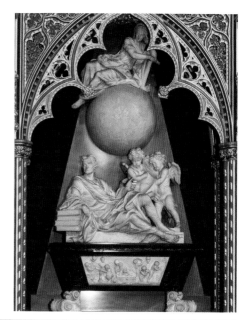

Right: Newton's tomb in Westminster Abbey, completed in 1731, uses Rococo fantasy to celebrate reason.

François Boucher

A central figure in Rococo painting, François Boucher (1703–70) was a favorite of the Marquise de Pompadour (1721–64), the mistress of Louis XV and a powerful figure at the French court at Versailles. (She was also an important patron of Enlightenment thinkers.) Boucher is celebrated for his sensuous female nudes, often presented in scenes from classical myth. His paintings have a lively dynamism based on flowing brushwork and pleasing colors. A joyous charm ripples through all his work.

Above: Boucher portrays the genteel comforts of his aristocratic patrons in The Luncheon Party *(1739).*

Jean-Honoré Fragonard

The shimmering lightness of touch makes *The Swing*, by Jean-Honoré Fragonard (1732–1806), the quintessential Rococo painting. It is a cunningly constructed piece, with light filtering through the idealized woodland to pick out the girl kicking off her slipper. The story continues with the lover in the undergrowth, and the man pulling at the swing in the mid-distance. The statues of cherubs underline the theme of love. A pupil of both Chardin and Boucher, Fragonard was hugely successful until the 1770s, when tastes changed.

Left: Everything about Fragonard's Swing *(1767) speaks of carefree fun and frivolity, dreamy love and luxury.*

Watteau
and the Age of Rococo

The rococo style was the product of a new mood of confidence in the 18th century, following the turmoil and religious conflict of the previous century. In painting, rococo artists turned away from weighty classical subjects and instead painted light, frothy scenes of pleasure, sensuality, and intimacy. The rococo was made popular by the work of a series of French artists working in and around Paris and the royal court at Versailles, starting with Jean-Antoine Watteau (1684–1721). By the end of the 18th century, however, the extravagant luxury that such paintings represented was one of the irritants that stirred ordinary French people into violent revolt against the royal family and privileged aristocracy. When the French Revolution swept them from power in 1789, the rococo style went with them.

Above: With its soft light and muted colors, Chardin's Boy with a Spinning Top *(1738) has a quiet intimacy that is another quality of the 18th century.*

Jean-Baptiste-Siméon Chardin

The paintings of Jean-Baptiste-Siméon Chardin (1699–1779) are works of quiet charm that are made harmonious by their delicately diffused light. He was evidently influenced by the paintings of the Le Nain brothers and of Dutch old masters such as de Hooch (see page 62). Instead of painting heroes and gods for the academy, Chardin unusually specialized in small canvases of still lifes or simple scenes of everyday life. After his success at the Paris Salon of 1737 he gained the favor of Louis XV and an international clientele.

Left: In Marie-Adelaide of France Represented As Diana *(1745), Nattier portrayed the fourth daughter of Louis XV as the Roman goddess of hunting.*

Right: Gainsborough was able to capture both the character of his sitters and their fashionable style, as seen in his Portrait of the Duchess of Beaufort, *painted in the 1770s.*

Mythological Identity

In the Rococo era, classical mythology was exploited as a mine of romantic possibilities—as witnessed in Watteau's *Embarkation for Cythera* (see below). In the fanciful world of Versailles, French aristocrats liked to play at assuming the identities of Greek and Roman gods. Louis XIV, for instance, had earlier associated himself with Apollo, in his role as the sun god. It is said that the Marquise de Pompadour posed for depictions of Venus for Boucher, and for the sculptor Étienne-Maurice Falconet (see page 72). With Jean-Marc Nattier (1685–1766), one of the most successful artists in the court of Louis XV, there was no secrecy: He made a number of portraits of aristocratic women clearly identified as classical goddesses.

Outside France

Nowhere quite captured the Rococo spirit of carefree frivolity and pleasure like Paris, but its mood filtered into the art of other countries. It can be detected, for instance, in the decorative schemes of Giambattista Tiepolo (1696–1770; see page 59) and fellow Venetian Jacopo Amigoni (c. 1685–1752), both of whom worked all over Europe. It can also be detected in the soaring ceiling frescoes of the Austrian painter Franz Anton Maulbertsch (1724–1796). In England, Thomas Gainsborough (1727–88) brought a light, shimmering elegance to his portraits of the aristocracy.

SHOWCASE: JEAN-ANTOINE WATTEAU, *THE EMBARKATION FOR CYTHERA*

The Embarkation for Cythera (or *Pilgrimage to the Island of Cythera,* 1717) is the painting that won Watteau a cherished place in the French academy and a title that represented a new type of artist: *peintre de fêtes galantes*—painter of the kind of elegant courtship party beloved of the French aristocracy, and so typical of the rococo era. Watteau painted dreamlike worlds of love and harmony, often based loosely on classical myth and touched with autumnal melancholy. The title suggests that the group is departing after a visit to Cythera, the island birthplace of Venus, goddess of Love.

Light, rapid brushstrokes give the painting an airy feel.

A stone herm depicting Venus has been garlanded with flowers.

Aerial perspective, as pioneered by Leonardo da Vinci, leads the eye off into the hazy blue of the far distance.

A swarm of cherubs, symbolic of love, flies off into the sky, away from the fanciful gilded boat.

Lovers turn back towards Venus's sacred grove, reluctant to leave.

The subject suggests a scene from the classical past, but the figures wear the elegant costume of a wealthy, more modern society.

Above: Piazza San Marco (c. 1760), a view of central Venice, shows how Guardi used a more atmospheric style than Canaletto.

Venice

One of the main destinations in Italy was Venice. Tourists went there to see the paintings of Bellini, Giorgione, Titian, and Veronese, to admire the architecture, to hear the music of Monteverdi and Marcello, to travel the canals in gondolas, to stay in the grand palazzi, and to enjoy the frenzied partying for which the city had become notorious. Various painters supplied them with pictures of Venice as souvenirs of their stay. The most celebrated was Giovanni Antonio Canal, called Canaletto (1697–1768), who painted captivating views of the city and its busy canals. His pupil Francesco Guardi (1712–93) painted similar scenes, but with a looser style that evokes well the unique light and atmosphere of Venice.

Above: This View of Paestum *(c. 1770–78) comes from a series of prints by Piranesi depicting the ruined temples at the ancient Greek settlement of Paestum, south of Naples.*

Postcards from the Grand Tour

During the 17th and 18th centuries, wealthy young English gentlemen traveled around Europe on journeys lasting up to five years. By visiting the main cultural sights, particularly in Italy (Venice, Florence, Rome, Pompeii), they intended to complete their education. Accompanied by tutors and guides, they learned about the art, architecture, history, and habits of Europe—and had a thoroughly enjoyable time. Then they returned home and decorated their houses with the antiquities, paintings, and other souvenirs they had acquired, to demonstrate their cultural achievements. Going on the "Grand Tour" became virtually essential for any fashionable young man, and by the 1780s as many as 40,000 tourists set out for Europe every year.

Above: A caricature depicts an art dealer selling a painting to a gullible Englishman on the Grand Tour. Tourists were a rich source of income and often victims of unscrupulous dealers.

Prints

By the 18th century, engravings and etchings had become a major feature of the art market. Knowledge of artists' work often spread abroad not so much through their paintings but through black-and-white prints of their paintings. Some artists only made prints. Among the tourists, there was a ready market for prints of the sights they had seen—the postcards of their day. Giovanni Battista Piranesi (1720–78) was a leading Italian printmaker, as well as an architect and an archeologist. His prints of the classical ruins were very popular. Purchasers cared little that they were romanticized and exaggerated for effect. Back home, collectors would frame the prints, or gather them in folders, to be admired at leisure.

Left: Canaletto was a master of broad city views, as seen in The Entrance to the Grand Canal, Venice *(c. 1730). He himself traveled widely in Europe and spent nine years in England, from 1746 to 1755.*

Artistic License

Canaletto, Guardi, and Pannini all indulged in capriccios (or "caprices")—paintings depicting a number of famous sights together, even though they were actually nowhere near each other. Pierre-Jacques Volaire (1729–c. 1802) was a French painter working in Rome and Naples. Mount Vesuvius, close to Naples, had four fairly major eruptions between 1760 and 1794, exciting the interest of the tourists, and Volaire painted more than 30 imaginative, moonlit versions of these events to fire their imaginations.

Portraits

One of the best souvenirs of the Grand Tour was a portrait, especially if made by one of the leading Italian portrait artists, such as Pompeo Batoni (1708–87), who worked in Rome. He knew exactly how to please his clients, painting them in a polished style, looking relaxed in their finery, with an admiring dog at their feet, and with a piece of classical architecture or sculpture close by to make them appear knowledgeable and cultured.

Left: This version of The Eruption of Vesuvius *in 1771 was painted by Volaire in 1779.*

Above: Portrait of John Staples *(1773) is a typical example of Batoni's finely painted portraits of English gentlemen on the Grand Tour.*

SHOWCASE: PANNINI, *THE GALLERY OF CARDINAL SILVIO VALENTI GONZAGA*

Giovanni Paolo Pannini (or Panini; 1691/2–1765) was famous for his views of Rome featuring the Roman ruins. He also painted scenes from contemporary Rome, including the interiors of theaters and galleries. This picture, painted in oil on canvas in 1749, depicts the kind of private gallery that young men on the Grand Tour would have been able to visit, but it exaggerates the palatial scale of the Gonzaga gallery.

Paintings are crammed onto the walls, in the manner that was usual for galleries at the time.

A number of the paintings are recognizable. The one hanging on the right side of the arch is a version of the *Portrait of Pope Leo X*, by Raphael.

Cardinal Silvio Valenti Gonzaga (1690-1756) was an art enthusiast who did much to preserve Rome's art collections. His own private collection numbered some 800 paintings. The artist is pictured standing next to the cardinal.

Students of art work at the desks.

William Hogarth

The English artist William Hogarth (1697–1764) used paintings to criticize and poke fun at contemporary society. He developed the idea of making sets of paintings to tell moral tales, rather like a modern comic strip. One of his best-known series is *A Rake's Progress* (1735), which tells the story, in eight separate scenes, of the wealthy young man Tom Rakewell, who wastes his fortune on luxuries, gambling, and partying, and ends up mad and ruined. Hogarth's vivid, sometimes cruel sense of humor can be found in the details, and in the caricaturelike depiction of the many characters.

Left: In an engraving of the second scene from Hogarth's A Rake's Progress, *Tom Rakewell is depicted recklessly spending his fortune.*

American Artists

The British colonies in North America were in a state of turmoil from the 1760s, and during the American Revolution leading to independence in 1783. They had close links with the French Enlightenment during this period. A number of American artists visited and worked in Europe. This included John Singleton Copley (1731–1815), who, in England, had considerable success with a new kind of painting: dramatic scenes from modern history, treated as earlier painters had depicted scenes from classical myth. Benjamin West (1738–1820) spent most of his career in England. A talented painter of elaborate historical scenes, he was a founding member of the Royal Academy. Many American painters came to know West in London, including John Trumbull (1756–1843), who is celebrated for his paintings of scenes from the American Revolution.

Below: Copley traveled in Italy with the wealthy American couple Mr. and Mrs. Ralph Izard, and in 1775 he painted their portrait (with the Colosseum in the background).

Paintings and Prints in the Age of Enlightenment

The Enlightenment shared with the Renaissance the same spirit of inquiry. Through reason and scientific analysis, it was argued, humanity should be able to solve many of the riddles of the universe, eradicate superstition and oppression, and find a means of living in harmony. France was an important center. Between 1751 and 1780 numerous contributors to the 35-volume *Encyclopédie* tried to reassess all knowledge in this new spirit. But when leveled at unjust systems of government, this kind of thinking led to revolt. Enlightenment principles inspired the American and French Revolutions.

Artists and Philosophers

Thinkers—known in France as *philosophes*—were the driving force of the Enlightenment. The editors of the *Encyclopédie*, Denis Diderot and Jean Le Rond d'Alembert, were among the leading philosophes. In their view, art played an important role in observing, analyzing, and recording the visual world: The *Encyclopédie* contained 3,129 illustrations. Thus artists had a key role to play in the Enlightenment. The philosophes also had a strong influence on what was considered good and bad art, and in France they helped to steer taste away from the Rococo and back toward the classical. With celebrity status, the leading thinkers were themselves portrayed in paintings and drawings. D'Alembert, for instance, was depicted in pastel by Maurice-Quentin de La Tour (1704–83).

Left: The celebrated German writer and thinker Johann Wolfgang von Goethe was portrayed by Johann Heinrich Tischbein (1751–1829) in 1787 in the countryside around Rome.

Above: Reynolds's dramatic Portrait of Mrs. Siddons As the Tragic Muse *(1784) shows this great actress accompanied by personifications of terror and pity.*

Pastel

Since the 16th century, artists had been using dry, chalklike sticks of powdered pigment mixed with gum to make drawings on paper or parchment. Originally they had three colors: white, black, and red. By the 18th century the color range had been extended and pastels became a popular medium, cherished for their soft, delicate finish, which could be enhanced by rubbing the lines. Some artists specialized in pastel, such as the Venetian-born portraitist Rosalba Carriera (1675–1757). She is credited with popularizing the technique in her travels across Europe, notably in France, where she influenced other leading exponents such as Maurice-Quentin de la Tour.

Joshua Reynolds

The late 18th century was a high point in the history of English portrait painting. One of the key figures in the field was Joshua Reynolds (1723–92), who painted his wealthy clients with precision, charm, and dignity. His portraits convey a strong notion of individuality, yet he also flattered his subjects with a sense of grandeur evoked by making them adopt classical poses, and through dramatic landscape backgrounds and the detail of their elegant costumes. Reynolds did much to enhance the status of artists in England: He was a founder and the first president of the Royal Academy, established in 1768, and was knighted the following year.

Below: The pastel drawing of a maid, called The Chocolate Girl *(c. 1744–45), is one of the best-known works by the Swiss-born artist Jean-Étienne Liotard (1702–89).*

SHOWCASE: JOSEPH WRIGHT, *THE ORRERY*

The English artist Joseph Wright (1734–97) is often referred to as Joseph Wright of Derby, after his hometown. With Caravaggesque chiaroscuro and clarity of detail, he painted startling images of England on the verge of the Industrial Revolution. His favorite themes included home scientists engaged with experiments and ironworkers at their forges. The full name of this painting, which dates from about 1766, is *A Philosopher Giving a Lecture on the Orrery*. An orrery was an instrument that demonstrated the movement of the planets around the sun.

The group is dramatically lit by an unseen light source in the middle of the orrery, blocked by the silhouetted child.

The main focus of the painting is the two boys, who are clearly enjoying the lecture as entertainment. Their inclusion carries the message that science is for everyone.

Wright often included women in his scenes of scientific experiment, even though, at the time, they had little access to scientific education.

One of the younger men attentively writes notes. The quality of Wright's painting can be seen in his portraiture.

Books on the shelf help to underline the atmosphere of study and learning.

Neoclassical
Painting and Sculpture

Excavations began at Herculaneum in 1738, and in 1748 in Pompeii—
Roman towns that had laid buried since the eruption of Vesuvius in 79 CE.
The discoveries reawakened interest in classical antiquity and encouraged a
more serious, academic approach in applying classical models to both art and
architecture. This new movement was called Neoclassicism—the "new classicism."
It was accompanied by a change of attitude that championed the perceived virtues
of ancient Greece and Rome, such as discipline, intellectual rigor, and patriotic courage.
This outlook and Neoclassical style appealed to the Enlightenment and to the new rulers
of revolutionary France, notably Napoleon, who rose to power in the 1790s and then began
a long campaign of conquest that engulfed Europe.

*Above: A marble relief sculpture of
the personification of day (1815),
with an awakened child,
demonstrates Thorvaldsen's
sentimental classicism.*

Jean-Auguste-Dominique Ingres
The two greatest exponents of
Neoclassical art were Jacques-Louis
David (see page 81) and his pupil
Jean-Auguste-Dominique Ingres
(1780–1867). In his early career
Ingres was a dedicated follower of
Neoclassicism, painting scenes from
classical myth in the same somewhat
stilted, sculptural style as his
master. Like David, he was drawn
into Napoleon's propaganda machine,
and he painted several portraits of
Napoleon, including one, in 1896,
with Napoleon seated on his throne
with all the pomp and glory of a
Roman emperor. After 1815 his
career suffered for a while from
this association with
Napoleon, but he returned
to fame with works of
nudes and sensual
scenes and
portraits of
great presence
and power.

Above: Ingres painted his Apotheosis of Homer
*in 1827 for a ceiling in the Louvre, returning to
neoclassical subject matter and style at the
height of his fame. Homer is seen presiding
over a gathering of writers and artists from
all of history.*

Bertel Thorvaldsen
The second-greatest Neoclassical
sculptor was Bertel Thorvaldsen
(1770–1844). A Dane brought up
and trained in Copenhagen, he
went to Rome in 1797 and
produced his famous *Jason*
(1802–03), a larger-than-life
marble statue of the hero in the
style of ancient Greek sculpture.
Thereafter he was much in demand
and ran a big workshop. Over his
career Thorvaldsen produced nearly
550 sculptures and was particularly
celebrated for his reliefs, depicting
both classical and religious
themes. He was hugely respected
in Denmark, where he returned in
1838, and in his lifetime a
museum was established for his
work and for his large collection of
paintings and antique sculpture.

Antonio Canova
Antonio Canova (1757–1822) was
the greatest Neoclassical sculptor.
Born in Italy, the son of a
stonemason, he worked mainly in
Rome, running a large studio that
took orders from all over Europe.
His style is graceful and
confident, with a distinctively
smooth and polished finish.
He depicted numerous
subjects from classical
mythology, taking ancient
Greek sculpture as his
model. One of his most
famous pieces is *The Three
Graces*, made in two
versions (1813–17).
Like Bernini (see pages
68–69), Canova wanted his
sculptures to be seen
from all angles, and even
arranged to have them
displayed on revolving
plinths.

*Right: Canova's
Venus Victrix
(Venus the
Conqueror;
1798–1805) is a
portrait of Pauline
Bonaparte, sister
of Napoleon, who
was married to a
member of the
Italian Borghese
family.*

The Rome Connection

Rome was a center for Neoclassical pilgrimage, where the German writer and archaeologist Johann Winckelmann (1717–68), the pope's superintendent of antiquities, played an influential role. His friend and compatriot in Rome, Anton Raffael Mengs (1728–79), adapted Winckelmann's ideas to produce early examples of Neoclassical religious and historical painting. He was also a portrait painter, rivaling Pompeo Batoni (see page 77). French artists had a direct link to the city through the Prix de Rome, a prestigious prize that provided a scholarship to study at the French Academy in Rome. Both David and Ingres won it, as did Anne-Louis Girodet de Roucy-Trioson (1767–1824), a pupil of David, who was in Rome from 1789 to 1795. Girodet-Trioson became known for his dramatic scenes from classical myth as well as his skilled portraits.

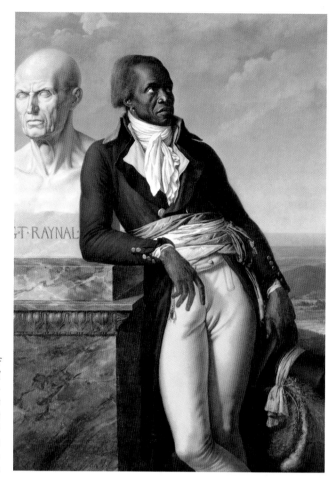

Left: It was assumed that the classical artists of antiquity had used muted and limited colors, and Mengs reflected this in his work, as seen in this Self-Portrait *(c. 1775).*

Right: The French slave colony of Haiti underwent a revolt in parallel with the French Revolution. Girodet-Trioson captures a new dignity in his portrait (1797) of the former slave Jean-Baptiste Mars Belley, deputy to the Convention in Paris. The bust is a portrait of Guillaume-Thomas Raynal, a contemporary antislavery reformer.

SHOWCASE: DAVID, *THE DEATH OF SOCRATES*

A pioneer and leader of French Neoclassical painting, Jacques-Louis David (1748–1825) developed a style designed to evoke all that was noble and elevating in classical antiquity. *The Death of Socrates* (1787) shows the moment when the great Greek philosopher took poison. Condemned for his teachings, Socrates was made to choose between renouncing his beliefs or death by poisoning. To the dismay of his followers, he chose the latter and undertook the task willingly for the benefit of knowledge.

In the background, Socrates' wife is depicted leaving the prison with other women.

Socrates' followers show a variety of expressions of grief. Only Plato, at the foot of the bed, and Crito, seated at his bedside, seem to control their emotions. The strongly modeled figures are arranged like a sculpted relief against a blank wall.

Socrates addresses the seated man, the only disciple who seems to accept his manner of death.

The chalice of poison is at the center of the picture, skillfully indicated by the strong gestures of Socrates and the disciple who reluctantly hands him the cup.

Like Ingres and Poussin (see pages 66–67), David uses a limited range of color in carefully balanced blocks. The yellow of this man's robe balances the fawn color of the bed.

Romanticism

Below: There is a raw horror in Goya's depiction of executions that had taken place in Madrid, titled Third of May, 1808 (painted in 1814).

Another, contrasting view of the world developed alongside Neoclassicism. In place of cool reason, discipline, and moral purpose, Romanticism championed feelings and moods, strong passions and fervor, spirituality, and the mysterious world of the unknown. The word *romanticism* was derived from imaginative medieval tales called romances. The movement was adopted enthusiastically by writers, composers, and artists. It took a number of forms, some of them seeming contradictory—idealizing both revolutionary fervor and serene, poetic beauty. In painting, artists moved away from the hard-edged, sculptural precision of Neoclassicism, favoring looser brushstrokes. References to the classical past were dropped in favor of modern themes and events.

Below: Friedrich's The Wanderer Above the Sea of Fog *(1818) expresses the awe of nature and the solitude of the Romantic poet.*

Political Content

The revolutions in America and France stirred deep passions and gave ordinary people a sense of power and possibility previously denied to them. Romantic artists and writers found much to admire in these events, sympathizing with the heroic gestures of the oppressed and downtrodden. They also protested against the horrors of war. Spain's greatest artist of the era, Francisco de Goya (1746–1828), was a court painter to the king, and he painted portraits and religious and historical works. But there was a darker side to his work. This came out in his reaction to the Napoleonic Wars that raged across Spain from 1808 to 1814, expressed most forcefully in his set of shockingly macabre engravings called *The Disasters of War* (1810–14).

Drama

The Romantics were drawn to the spectacular—events that put the very nature of existence to the test. One of the greatest and most controversial paintings of the time was *The Raft of the Medusa*, a huge canvas by the French artist Théodore Géricault (1791–1824), which illustrated a recent news story. It depicts the desperate survivors of a French frigate shipwrecked in 1816, whose fate was blamed on social injustice and government incompetence. It was the first time a contemporary event had been made the subject of art in this grand style. The Romantics also found drama in nature, and the artist who most consistently captured this attitude was the German Caspar David Friedrich (1774–1840).

Below: Géricault's Raft of the Medusa *(1818-19) is impressive also for its sheer scale: It is more than 23 feet (7 m) wide.*

The World of William Blake

Poet, artist, illustrator, visionary, and mystic William Blake (1757–1827) was a unique character among the English Romantics and was considered an eccentric by some and a genius by others. He began as an engraver and illustrated his own books of poetry and prose, hand-engraving the lettering and using a method of color printing that he had developed himself. He also did watercolors and used tempera, but refused to use oil on canvas. He had a highly individual style, showing a greater admiration for Gothic art and Michelangelo than for his contemporaries. All his work was colored by his strong spirituality, which was reinforced, apparently, by visions and messengers from heaven. He believed that the world of the imagination was reality and that the material world was "but a faint shadow." Living close to poverty, he was supported by friends and patrons and, toward the end of his life, had a group of devoted younger admirers.

Fantasy

The world of dreams and the imagination was fascinating to the Romantics. Often this was expressed with a macabre twist. Between 1819 and 1824, Goya shut himself away in a house outside Madrid and painted 14 fiercely worked and nightmarish murals, called his "Black Paintings," featuring demons, monsters, and witches. A Swiss-born painter working in England, Henry Fuseli (1741–1825) was a friend and supporter of Blake, and painted equally imaginative works—dark and theatrically lit, and often deeply unsettling, such as *The Nightmare* (1782). But unlike Blake, Fuseli belonged in the mainstream of art and taught at the Royal Academy.

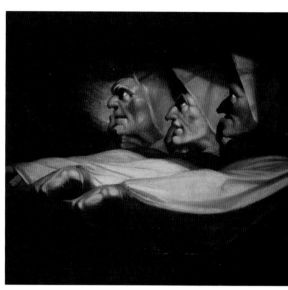

Above: Blake's etching The Ancient of Days *was used as the frontispiece of his illustrated book* Europe, a Prophecy *(1794). It depicts God designing the universe with mathematical precision.*

Right: In Three Witches *(1783), Fuseli gives his interpretation of the abominable characters of Shakespeare's play* Macbeth.

SHOWCASE: DELACROIX, *LIBERTY LEADING THE PEOPLE*

All classes took part in the July Revolution. The man in the top hat represents the middle classes.

The central figure is a personification of liberty. She holds the French flag, the *tricolore*, which was closely associated with the French Revolution of 1789.

Liberty is also wearing the Phrygian cap, another symbol of the French Revolution, and as worn by the female emblem of France, called Marianne.

The stance of Liberty may well have inspired Frédéric-Auguste Bartholdi when he designed the Statue of Liberty in the 1880s (see page 98).

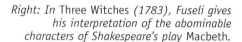

Eugène Delacroix (1798–1863) ranks as one of the two leading French Romantic painters, alongside his friend Géricault (who died in a riding accident at the age of just 33). Using a brisk, dynamic style, he depicted passionate scenes of drama and war, as well as portraits and exotic Eastern and North African scenes. *Liberty Leading the People* (1830) commemorates the July Revolution that took place that same year in Paris, overthrowing the unpopular King Charles X.

The twin towers of Notre Dame Cathedral of Paris can be seen in the background (see page 35).

The triangular shape of the composition, reinforced by the smoke, helps to convey the uplifting sense of triumph.

The bodies signify the suffering and sacrifice that are the cost of achieving liberty.

Romantic Landscape

Landscape painting took on a new significance during the Romantic era. Romantics held a strong belief that landscape could directly affect one's mood, and they looked for ways to experience an emotional interaction with nature. Landscape could be simply serene, beautiful, and charming, or it could be awe-inspiring and sublime, expressing the vastness and power of nature. Between these two lay the picturesque: landscape that was beautiful but had a curious and arresting irregularity in the composition of its elements. These were subjects that were much written about and discussed at the time. Landscape paintings for sale and exhibition were still created in the studio, but increasingly artists were making oil sketches outdoors.

Above: Constable's famous "six-footer" The Hay Wain *(1821) caused a sensation when exhibited in Paris in 1824.*

John Constable
One of the greatest English landscape painters, John Constable (1775–1837) worked initially around his home in Dedham Vale in Suffolk. Born the son of a miller, he knew this landscape intimately, along with the activities of all the people living in it, and his deep love of it shines through. Constable's most ambitious pieces were his "six-footers"—large canvases 6 feet (1.8 m) wide. In these, he used dabs and flecks of paint, notably white to imitate the sparkle of light, which gave the impression of freshness and immediacy, and a sense of the changing weather. Nonetheless, his large, studio-finished paintings have a somewhat contrived and labored feel to them, while his many sketches and his smaller paintings have greater vitality and spontaneity. He was almost exactly the same age as the other great English landscape painter of the day, J. M. W. Turner (see page 85), who was more successful professionally.

Above: The title of Corot's Recollections of Mortefontaine *(1864) tells us that this was not a faithful study of a landscape but an idealized memory.*

The Barbizon School and Corot
In the 1840s to 1860s, a group of French painters lived and worked in the village of Barbizon, in the forest of Fontainebleau, outside Paris. Théodore Rousseau (1812–67) and Charles-François Daubigny (1817–78) and their many associates set out to document landscapes that expressed a romantic view of nature—charming for its unspoiled and natural beauty. Constable was one of their main inspirations. Woodlands, heaths, and streams were their typical subjects, painted in somber greens and russet colors. Another French artist associated with the Barbizon school was Jean-Baptiste-Camille Corot (1796–1875). In his landscapes he generally has a less idealized approach (see page 89), but in the 1850s he began painting woodland scenes caught in the silvery light of dawn or dusk—very much in the Romantic tradition.

Right: The Cross in the Wilderness *(1845), by Thomas Cole, was inspired by a poem of that name by the British poet Felicia Hemans.*

Literary Influences
The Romantic movement was driven, above all, by literature. New sensibilities toward nature were expressed in works such as *Reveries of a Solitary Walker* (published in 1782), by the Swiss-French Enlightenment philosopher Jean-Jacques Rousseau. In England, a key work was the collection of poems *Lyrical Ballads* (1798), by the "Lake Poets" William Wordsworth and Samuel Taylor Coleridge, who lived for a while in the beautiful Lake District of northwest England. This collection included Wordsworth's famous celebration of natural beauty, "Tintern Abbey." Such works helped to shape the poetic mindset of Romantic landscape painters. For instance, in the United States this was seen in the work of Thomas Cole (1801–48), a leading figure in the Hudson River school (see page 88).

Above: Turner's Burning of the House of Lords and Commons *(1835) was based on sketches he had made of the real event the year before.*

Joseph Mallord William Turner

Joseph Mallord William Turner (1775–1851) was a prodigiously gifted painter. The son of a barber, his talent was spotted at an early age, and he was trained at the Royal Academy Schools in London. He made his name with technically brilliant landscapes, architectural studies, historical paintings, and exhilarating seascapes in the style of the old Dutch masters. Turner traveled widely in Europe, always busily sketching and picking up ideas from other artists; in landscape, Claude Lorrain (see page 66) became a major inspiration. At the age of about 32, he began to experiment with his landscapes and seascapes, using sweeping, expressive brushstrokes and unreal colors, so that the detail of the subject matter became less important than the play of light and the general mood of the scene. These experiments were not much appreciated at the time but had a major impact on artists later in the century.

Symbolic Imagery

The paintings of Caspar David Friedrich are more than just scenes: They have symbolic meaning—but that meaning is often not clear. *The Sea of Ice*, for instance, is thought perhaps to be symbolic of the crushed hopes of Europe, still—in 1824—suffering in the aftermath of the Napoleonic Wars. In an earlier work, *Dolmen in the Snow* (c. 1807), Friedrich depicts a lonely prehistoric dolmen (rock shelter), surrounded by three trees. The dolmen could represent paganism or a tomb, and the three trees Christianity, as in the three crosses at the crucifixion of Christ. If so, what is the relationship between them? Is this an allegory of the wintry bleakness of death before the Resurrection? We are left to wonder. Romantic landscape paintings often seem to refer to ideas beyond what they depict.

Above: There is a haunting spirituality to Friedrich's Dolmen in the Snow, *which invites speculation about its intended symbolism.*

SHOWCASE: FRIEDRICH, *THE SEA OF ICE*

Caspar David Friedrich was one of the great painters of the sublime type of Romantic landscape art (see page 82). His subject matter does not seem invented or contrived, but he has a way of inserting a sense of menacing and mysterious power, sometimes underlined by shadowy figures, or troubling, symbolic detail—such as the wreckage of a ship in *The Sea of Ice* (1824).

The ice has been shattered by the awesomely destructive force of nature into outlandish, jagged chunks.

The stern of the wrecked sailing ship is an indication of the huge scale of the ice.

Scattered broken masts lie trapped in the ice, as if being devoured by it.

The broken slabs of rock in the foreground, echoing the shapes of the ice, place the viewer on a shore.

Above: In The Gleaners *(1857), Millet depicts the traditional job of collecting loose grain that has fallen onto the ground during harvesting. The women labor silently in their backbreaking task.*

Jean-François Millet

With industrialization and the growth of the cities, the countryside was changing fast, and life for poor farmers had become very hard. The French painter Jean-François Millet (1814–75) came from a rural peasant family, and he captured the dignity and hardship of this life in a series of paintings. Glowing with soft color, they show a warm affection for the traditional farming lifestyle, tinged with sadness. Millet was closely associated with the Barbizon school of landscape painters (see page 84), but he took a distinctive path, finding a way of applying the grand style of Poussin and Lorrain (see pages 66–67) to scenes of the rural life of his day.

Realism

By the mid-19th century, the Western world was undergoing the radical changes of industrialization and the rapid growth of cities and the middle classes. A new generation of artists searched for ways to express the realities of this changed world. Why not, they thought, just paint the world as it really is? Artists had, of course, depicted the real world in the past, such as the Dutch painters of the 17th century (see pages 62–63), but they had manipulated it to express either symbolism, harmony, or humor. The 19th-century realists took a more direct approach, painting the realities of the ordinary modern world—a subject that had not previously been considered appropriate for art.

Above right: Eakins was fascinated by anatomy and attended dissection classes and live operations. The Gross Clinic (1875) shows Dr. Gross performing an operation.

Right: Manet's large painting The Fifer *(1866) was controversial for its bold use of flat areas of color and almost complete absence of background.*

Édouard Manet

By this time, France had become the trendsetter in art, and realism was driven forward by a number of radical painters. But their new approach was still guided by studying the history of art. Édouard Manet (1832–83) searched for lessons in the work of the old masters, such as Titian, Velázquez, and Goya. He applied these to pictures of modern life, using a technique of bold brushstrokes to give his work a lively sense of immediacy. By transferring historical attitudes about nudes in art to modern-day subjects, as in *Le Déjeuner sur l'Herbe* (*Luncheon on the Grass*, 1863), he caused a public scandal but won the approval of younger artists.

Thomas Eakins

French Realism was a major inspiration to Thomas Eakins (1844–1916), one of the greatest American painters, who studied in Paris in 1866–70. Applying his firm belief in depicting faithfully what he saw, without sentimentality, he painted powerful portraits, figures in landscapes, and uncustomary subjects such as wrestling matches and surgeons at work. Eakins was also a keen photographer, exploring this new way of recording the real world.

The Danish School

Denmark enjoyed a golden age of painting in the early 19th century, when a number of gifted artists chose to depict Danish subjects. A leading figure was Christoffer Wilhelm Eckersberg (1783–1853), who brought clean and pure form of Neoclassicism to portraits and landscape. His many pupils included Christen Købke (1810–48), the outstanding Danish painter of his generation, who adapted Eckersberg's disciplined style to paint well-observed, realistic images of the world.

Below: In the oil painting The Third-Class Carriage *(1863–65), Daumier sketches a grim view of the reality of railway travel, a wonder of the modern age.*

Left: Much of Købke's work depicts his family and friends, such as this portrait of the landscape painter Frederik Sødring (1832).

Honoré Daumier

The French painter Honoré Daumier (1808–79) used powerful caricature and satire to mock and criticize the modern world. His drawings (made into prints) poked fun at current events and politicians, lawyers, and the wealthy. His paintings used a similar vigorous and exaggerated style to depict movingly the hardships of the working classes, ground down by poverty and physical labor. Even when painting in oil, he used a sketchy style, with strong lines, scratchy and thin layers of paint, and somber colors.

SHOWCASE: COURBET, *THE WINNOWERS*

A central figure in the development of Realism was the French painter Gustave Courbet (1819–77). A man of radical beliefs and great self-assurance, he campaigned vigorously for Realism. In his paintings of scenes from ordinary life, he often showed a strong sympathy for the hardships of ordinary working people. *The Winnowers* (1854) depicts rural women at the task of separating grain from the chaff (husks and bits of straw).

This is not a painting of misery. The sacks of grain are full, and the figures look well dressed and well fed.

The pose of the girl using the sieve is strong and dignified as if inspired by Michelangelo.

The attitude of the girl sorting grain on a dish suggests the tedium of the task.

The scene appears composed in pieces like a mosaic of separate snapshots. The figures, especially the boy opening the box, are not communicating with each other.

Realistic Landscape

The Romantics had sought an emotional engagement with landscape. They wanted to swoon at its sheer beauty or be stunned by its heartless power. The Realists wanted to show landscape as it really was, without interpreting it or laying any meaning on it. To be worth painting, a landscape had to be striking in some way: For the realist, it was a question of selecting a view and then making an accurate record of it, and showing why it was striking, without bending the truth to manufacture an effect. Realist painters used bright colors and urgent brushstrokes to capture the vitality of the scene.

Above: George Inness (1825–94) painted in the style of the Hudson River school but used a softer touch in order to evoke atmosphere, as seen in The Rainbow *(c. 1878).*

Above: For Twilight in the Wilderness *(1860), Frederic Edwin Church combined a series of landscape sketches from Maine and New York with sunsets he witnessed in New York City.*

The Hudson River School

In the United States a loosely defined group of artists known as the Hudson River school set out to capture the unique beauty of the American landscape. Their name refers to the Hudson River in New York State, in an area that Thomas Cole (see page 84) began to paint in 1825. Over time, members of the group gradually spread out across North America into the spectacular landscapes that were only just being discovered by pioneers moving west from the East Coast states. Other artists associated with the group include Asher Durand (1796–1886) and Thomas Doughty (1783–1856) and, later, Frederic Edwin Church (1826–1900) and Albert Bierstadt (1830–1902). They combined immense technical skill with an acutely poetic sensitivity to produce work of startling power and—in the case of Bierstadt—almost photographic precision. Their strong emphasis on the play of light, brilliantly rendered by meticulous brushwork, was later labeled Luminism. Much of their work was romanticized, such as scenes of deer drinking from mountain lakes in misty sunsets. For this reason it is sometimes referred to as "Romantic Realism."

Winslow Homer

Whereas the Hudson River school explored America's majestic wildernesses, Winslow Homer (1836–1910) painted far more intimate scenes of his homeland—ordinary people living, working, and playing in their own landscapes. Homer is also celebrated for his seascapes and marine paintings, mostly produced from his home in Maine, where he lived on Prout's Neck, a peninsula in Scarborough. But he went to Paris for a year in 1867, and lived in the fishing village of Cullercoats in Northumberland, northeast England, for two years (1881–82)— an experience that reignited his boyhood love of the sea.

Right: Winslow Homer is celebrated for his pictures of children enjoying the outdoor adventures, bright weather, and leisure of long summer days. Boys in a Pasture *(1874) is a famous example.*

SHOWCASE: COURBET, *YOUNG WOMEN FROM THE VILLAGE*

Gustave Courbet liked to court controversy, producing large-scale paintings of ordinary people, often from his hometown of Ornans. When *Young Women from the Village* was first exhibited in 1852, critics called it ugly because it contradicted all the notions of romantic beauty: The landscape is scrappy, the women look common, and the subject is unsettling. For Courbet, this was reality, which had its own kind of beauty.

The women are dressed for a country walk, shading their faces from the sun.

One of the young women hands a gift of money to the poor cowgirl. The gesture is unsentimental—everyone looks rather awkward about it.

The three women are in fact portraits of Courbet's three sisters, Zélie, Juliette, and Zoé.

Corot's Realism

Below: Corot's Florence: View from the Boboli Gardens resulted from his second trip to Italy in 1834. In the center is Brunelleschi's dome (see page 43).

The French painter Jean-Baptiste-Camille Corot produced many landscapes in the Romantic tradition, especially after the 1840s (see page 84). But earlier in his career, he developed another style, notably after the first of several trips to Italy in 1825. Essentially realistic, he produced captivating small paintings of rural views and villages, applying muted, dry colors to evoke the warmth of the weather. His close observation of light suggests that this is just how the scene looked at a particular time of day. Millet (see page 86) and Courbet both conveyed strong sentiments in their landscapes. Corot was a more dispassionate observer, sketching what he saw in front of him and making it significant through the way he selected the composition of the view in the finished painting.

Right: Ferdinand Georg Waldmüller painted studies of trees almost as if they were portraits, as seen in Elm Trees in the Prater *(1831).*

Nature

The study of nature in art academies became a source of conflict. Many of the old academics (see page 90) believed that the skills of painting should be learned from the study of the work of the old masters and by copying plaster casts of Greek sculpture. The new generation of Realists insisted on the study of nature (including live nude models from the start) without idealizing it. The Austrian Ferdinand Georg Waldmüller (1793–1865) lost his job as professor of painting at the Vienna Academy in 1857 over the issue of nature. His belief in the value of observing nature in the closest detail can be detected in his landscapes.

Academics
and Pre-Raphaelites

During most of the 19th century, the art world was dominated by the academies. These were the old and much respected teaching institutions for "fine art." They also ran important exhibitions every year, selecting the best work submitted to them, and in this way they were the guardians of standards and good taste. Some had been doing this for a long time: The French Royal Academy of Painting and Sculpture had been set up in 1648, and London's Royal Academy of Arts was established in 1768. "Academic art" tended to be work that was technically excellent and dealt with traditional subject matter: historical and religious scenes, portraits, landscapes, and still lifes. The academies were cautiously open to new art movements, but they aroused vehement criticism by exhibiting controversial work, such as the realist paintings of Gustave Courbet and Édouard Manet (see pages 86–89).

Above: The Sword Dance *(c. 1870) was the kind of work that the French academy favored, and the artist, Jean-Léon Gérôme (1824–1904), was a staunch defender of academic traditions.*

The French Salon

Each year the French academy held a huge and influential exhibition of new paintings called the Salon. Thousands of pieces of work were submitted for selection. Much hung on the decision of the selection committee: Artists could make their name—and a living—if their work was chosen for exhibition. But by the 1860s new approaches to painting were beginning to challenge the artistic taste of the academy. In 1863 the selection committee rejected so many new paintings that there was an uproar, and the ruler of France, Napoléon III, decided to step in and create a special exhibition of rejected work, the Salon des Refusés. The event was famous for the passions it aroused: Critics raged about works such as Manet's *Le Déjeuner sur l'Herbe* (see page 86), and the public turned up simply to scoff and mock.

The Old Guard

Many of the French academic painters fiercely resisted the new trend toward realism. Their kind of painting depended on great natural talent, years of training, and enormous amounts of patience. By the 1860s, they felt that all the traditional values of fine art were under threat from painters who opposed everything they stood for. One notable artist of the old guard was Adolphe-William Bouguereau (1825–1905), painter of religious, historical, and sentimental scenes. For the last 50 years of his life, he faced growing opposition from younger artists in the schools and salons—but the general public, at least, was largely on his side.

Left: The Dutch-born artist Lawrence Alma Tadema (1836–1912) came to England in 1870 and became known for the beautifully rendered detail of his work, as seen in The Finding of Moses by the Pharaoh's Daughter *(1904).*

In England

The academic tradition of highly polished technique was upheld by a number of leading artists in England. Frederick Leighton (1830–96) painted finely worked classical scenes rich in detail. William Powell Frith (1819–1909), by contrast, painted contemporary scenes packed with characters and detail, such as *Derby Day* (1878), which fascinated huge, enthusiastic crowds at the Royal Academy. The French artist James Tissot (1836–1902) also had a major impact in London. Having exhibited in the Paris Salon since the age of 23, he lived in England from 1871 to 1882, producing exquisitely made pictures of beautifully dressed Victorian high society, painted with almost photographic precision—realism for the upper classes.

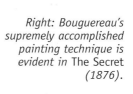

Right: Bouguereau's supremely accomplished painting technique is evident in The Secret *(1876).*

The Pre-Raphaelites

In 1848 a group of English artists formed the Pre-Raphaelite Brotherhood, claiming that art had gone wrong since the time of the Renaissance artist Raphael. Many Pre-Raphaelites were inspired by the delicacy and preciousness of the Florentine early Renaissance artists Filippino Lippi and Botticelli. Others admired the precision of Jan van Eyck. From this they evolved a distinctive style of their own: elaborate, detailed, and highly colored. The founders were William Holman Hunt (1825–1910), Dante Gabriel Rossetti (1828–82), and John Everett Millais (1829–96). They shared a romantic belief in the virtues of the medieval world and the horrors of industrialization.

Left: In La Ghirlandata *(The Woman with a Garland, 1873), Rossetti painted William Morris's wife, Jane, whose distinctive looks became a model of beauty.*

Right: Every inch of The Blind Girl *(1856), by John Everett Millais, is painted in intricate detail, down to the strands of hair and the blades of grass.*

Sentiment

The Pre-Raphaelites painted mainly religious and historical classical subjects, or contemporary scenes with strong moral messages. Often the content oozed with sickly and sweet sentiment, but this was not unusual in Victorian art or literature. The same applied to the work of Bouguereau, whose art included throngs of perfect angels and kissing cherubs. Millais' *The Blind Girl* is very sentimental, with a blatantly obvious message: All these wonders of the visual world—the rainbow, the pretty rural scene, the butterfly on her shawl—are lost on her, but the positive feel of the painting suggests that she will be rewarded with sight in the next life. This painting serves as a reminder that tastes in art change over time.

SHOWCASE: WILLIAM HOLMAN HUNT, *THE FINDING OF THE SAVIOR IN THE TEMPLE*

William Holman Hunt was one of the leading figures in the Pre-Raphaelite Brotherhood (see above). He was noted for his highly detailed, richly colored work, often sentimental in content. *The Finding of the Savior in the Temple* (1854–62) shows the scene in which the parents of 12-year-old Jesus, after three days of searching, find him in the Temple of Jerusalem talking to learned teachers. This painting was a huge popular success.

It was shocking to some critics that Hunt should bring such realism to a biblical scene, especially his portrayal of the young Christ and his parents as ordinary people.

The picture is full of symbolism. For instance, a temple outside is being built, just as Christ will build a new religion. But the scaffolding also forms a cross.

Hunt made the first of several visits to the Holy Land in 1854 and looked for authentic details, such as the architectural screens in the background.

The old blind rabbi clutches the holy Jewish scriptures discussed daily in the temple.

Impressionism

A number of the artists who had exhibited in the notorious Salon des Refusés in Paris in 1863 (see page 90) continued to work together, sharing new, radical ideas about painting. They were realists, but they were not interested in grim reality. Instead, they wanted to paint the aspects of the modern world that appealed to them, and to capture the fleeting moment of the present. To do this they painted outdoors, working quickly, using rapid brushstrokes and dabs of unmixed color. Critics complained that their paintings looked unfinished—that they were just "impressions."

Right: Frédéric Bazille (1841–70) joined other Impressionists painting outdoors, capturing the play of light in paintings like Summer Scene *(1869).*

Painting Outdoors
In the past, it had not been easy to do oil painting outdoors: The paints and equipment were just too cumbersome. But in the 1840s, paint manufacturers learned how to put oil paint into small tubes, which were easy to carry around. Suddenly the possibility of painting outdoors became practical. At first, artists used these paints to make oil sketches outdoors but still did the finished painting in the studio. But the Impressionists realized that they could catch the immediate, spontaneous sense of weather in a landscape—and the effect of light at different moments of the day—only by painting the finished work on the spot, outdoors (*en plein air,* in French). The Impressionists became avid *plein air* painters, prepared to work in all weather conditions.

Above: Berthe Morisot (1841–95) was the only woman to show work in the first Impressionist exhibition. She painted The Butterfly Hunt *later that year.*

Above: Degas applied his unusual approach to composition in his many paintings of race courses, such as At the Races in the Countryside *(1869).*

The Exhibition of 1874
Paris was thrown into chaos by the French defeat in the Franco-Prussian War (1870–71) and the doomed revolutionary Paris Commune that followed. Many of the radical young artists fled abroad, several to England. After their return, they found their art was still rejected by the official Salon, and so in April 1874 a group of about 30 of them mounted their own exhibition. It aroused outrage from many critics, and ridicule from the public. One critic, picking on a sketchy painting called *Impression: Sunrise,* by Claude Monet (1840–1926), scornfully branded the group "impressionists." They rather liked this, and called themselves Impressionists from then on. There were eight such Impressionist exhibitions between 1874 and 1886 and over that period the artists established their reputations and became increasingly accepted into the mainstream.

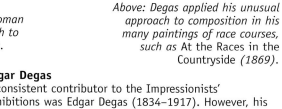

Below: In a cartoon of 1874, a policeman warns a pregnant woman that it is dangerous for her health to enter the impressionist exhibition.

Edgar Degas
A consistent contributor to the Impressionists' exhibitions was Edgar Degas (1834–1917). However, his painting took a somewhat different course. He was more interested in figure work than in landscapes, and did not paint outdoors. In the 1860s, Japanese prints began to reach Europe, and Degas was fascinated by the originality of their quirky compositions, with main elements of the composition running into the frame. He used this off-center kind of composition to give a spark of immediacy to his pictures, as though seeing a scene in an accidental glance. Like the other Impressionists, he was strongly influenced by the work of Édouard Manet (see page 86), and, like Manet, Degas continued to use black in his paintings after the Impressionists had rejected it as unnatural, favoring deep shades of primary colors instead.

SHOWCASE: MONET, *POPPIES AT ARGENTEUIL*

Claude Monet was one of the leading figures of Impressionism. He painted *Poppies at Argenteuil* in 1873 and showed it at the first Impressionist exhibition the following year. Many aspects of the picture are typical of Impressionist painting: the rapid brushstrokes, the modern subject matter, the powerful evocation of the weather, and the artist's sheer delight in the beauty of the scene.

Monet has used his wife, Camille, and son Jean as models, not once but twice.

Monet paints the long, dry grasses in the mid-distance as a misty haze.

The Impressionists liked to use complementary colors based on the three primary colors (red, blue, and yellow). Red is complementary to green (a mixture of yellow and blue). The poppies are painted as dabs of unmixed red.

Jean has been painted very sketchily: The hand holding a bunch of poppies is merely a flesh-colored blob.

Pierre-Auguste Renoir

Pierre-Auguste Renoir (1841–1919) was a key member of the Impressionist group and became the best known of all of them during his lifetime. He started his career in Limoges as a porcelain painter—decorating ceramics. In 1862 he went to Paris to study art with the academic painter Charles Gleyre (1808–74), and there he formed close friendships with fellow students Bazille, Monet, and Alfred Sisley (1839–99). They often painted together *en plein air*, excitedly forging the principles of Impressionism. During these early years, he lived in poverty. Renoir soon adapted the Impressionist technique to paint pictures of Parisians at leisure—at the theater, in cafés, dining, dancing. Through such work, focusing on the pleasures of life, he captured an upbeat spirit of the time, and by the 1880s his painting had become very popular.

Gustave Caillebotte

Born into a wealthy family, Gustave Caillebotte (1848–94) generously helped the Impressionists through their early days of poverty by giving them money and buying their paintings (38 of these are now in the Musée d'Orsay in Paris). He was himself a gifted artist, producing polished, realist paintings of Paris life, with deliberately casual composition reminiscent of photography. He was particularly skilled at reproducing shiny surfaces. Caillebotte contributed paintings to five of the eight Impressionist exhibitions.

Right: Caillebotte gives a very ordinary name to Paris Street; Rainy Day *(1877), but it is made special by the rain-washed streets, and the unusual, fish-eye perspective of the background.*

Left: Dance at the Moulin de la Galette *(1876) displays Renoir's fascination with the light as it filters through the trees. The scene is the outdoor courtyard of a popular Sunday-afternoon dance venue in Montmartre, a suburb of Paris.*

Monet's Waterlilies
Monet remained a passionate experimenter throughout his long life. During the 1890s he painted several series of paintings—of haystacks, and the Cathedral of Rouen, for example—to show how the light changed at different times of the day and in different seasons. He developed the large garden at his house in Giverny and became fascinated by the play of light on the waterlilies and water. In 1918, in his late 70s, he undertook a commission to paint huge canvases of these waterlilies, which were later permanently installed in their own rooms in the Orangerie gallery in Paris.

Left: Waterlilies: Morning *is one of eight huge canvases on this subject painted by Monet between 1920 and his death in 1926.*

Late Impressionism

By the 1880s, Impressionism had become well established in France, and soon artists all over Europe—as well as the United States, Australia, and Japan—were eagerly adopting the style. The main Impressionist painters who had created this revolution now pursued their own paths, some remaining close to Impressionism's original goals, others moving in new directions. Photography was beginning to present a real challenge to painting. Although still entirely black-and-white, it could portray the real world with a penetrating immediacy. So the Impressionists explored aspects of art where photography could not compete—in the study of the effects of light on color, for instance.

Degas' Dancers
Ballet dancers were a major source of inspiration for Edgar Degas (see also page 92). He drew and painted them tirelessly throughout his career. Most of his ballet dancers are not performing onstage—rather, they are rehearsing, or waiting to go onstage, or resting, caught in private thought. Degas painted them in oil and gouache, but he was also a master of pastel, using the soft colors and blurred edges to convey movement.

Right: Degas' pastel Four Ballerinas Behind the Scenes *(c. 1899) shows the dancers limbering up to go onstage.*

Above: Boulevard Montmartre: Afternoon, Sunshine *is one of four that Pissarro painted of this view in 1897, with changing times of day and weather.*

Camille Pissarro
Born and raised in the West Indies, Camille Pissarro (1830–1903) was some ten years older than the other impressionists and acted like a father figure to them. He helped to evolve the impressionist style, was a driving force behind the impressionist exhibitions, and was the only one to show work in all eight. Pissarro was a gifted landscape painter, brilliantly using the impressionist technique to convey the feel of the weather. He also applied these skills to city streets. He continued to paint in the impressionist style for most of his life.

SHOWCASE: CÉZANNE, *MONT SAINTE-VICTOIRE AND THE VIADUCT*

The bare peak of Mont Sainte-Victoire was a major landmark near Cézanne's home in Aix-en-Provence, in southern France.

Cézanne used a hatching technique of short parallel lines to evoke slight movement in the branches of the pine trees.

The fields and farm buildings create an abstract pattern of rectangles, which contrast with the rounded shapes in the trees.

Paul Cézanne (1839–1906) was a close associate of the Impressionists and showed work in the impressionist exhibitions of 1874 and 1877. He painted outdoors, but he never fully adopted the Impressionist technique. Looking for a more solid sense of structure in landscape, he tended to break his paintings up into blocks of color and shapes, searching for satisfactory relationships between them. He painted Mont Sainte-Victoire repeatedly; this view dates from 1885–87.

The tubelike verticals of the tree trunks are counterbalanced by the strong horizontal structure of the viaduct.

The winding road leads the eye into the picture.

American Impressionists in Paris

Paris was the center of the Western art world, and various American artists who went there in the 1870s and 1880s were touched by the fervor for impressionism. Through her friendship with Degas, the American artist Mary Cassatt (1844–1926) became a close associate of the Impressionists and showed her work in their exhibitions. She came from a wealthy family and lent the Impressionist painters valuable financial support. In her own art she specialized in paintings of women and children—charming and beautiful, without being sentimental. The American-born portrait artist John Singer Sargent (1856–1925) went through an intense Impressionist period between 1884 and 1889 as he developed the elegant, updated academic style for which he is famous.

Below: Mary Cassatt's mastery of the Impressionist technique can be seen in the soft, sweeping brushstrokes and color contrasts in Young Woman Sewing in the Garden *(c. 1880–82).*

Left: The influence of Impressionism is still evident in John Singer Sargent's An Artist in His Studio, *painted in 1904.*

Postimpressionism

The Postimpressionists broke the mold of Western art. For centuries artists had sought to make pictures that resembled windows opening onto real views of the world. Impressionism recognized the extraordinary variety of colors, light, and shadows in the visual world. The next generation of artists, especially those at the center of the feverish art scene in France, now looked to see what else their art could express. Their experiments took them in a multitude of directions, all falling under the broad label of Postimpressionism.

Above: One of Rousseau's last works, Jungle with Horse Attacked by a Jaguar *(1910) portrays a strange, dreamlike world, painted with meticulous care.*

Above: Gauguin's Two Tahitian Women and a Dog *(1893) is typical of his late work, boldly flattened in composition, glowing with vivid color, and full of poetic mystery.*

Paul Gauguin

Having spent his childhood in Peru, Paul Gauguin (1848–1903) worked in Paris as a successful stockbroker. He started painting as a hobby but began to take it more seriously in 1874, when he met Pissarro. In 1883 he gave up his job and moved to Pont-Aven in Brittany, where he developed a new style of painting using strong outlines filled with bright, flat color, and rather naive (childlike) figures. Gauguin took part in the last four Impressionist exhibitions but struggled to make a living. In 1891 he went to live on the French Polynesian island of Tahiti, in the South Pacific. There he introduced aspects of Polynesian art into his painting and sculpture, and produced the work for which he is best remembered—but he was virtually unknown at the time of his death.

Below: Seurat's Sunday Afternoon on the Island of La Grande Jatte *(1884–86) is a huge painting 10 feet (3 m) wide. It has the static quality and peculiar silence found in much of Seurat's work.*

Le Douanier Rousseau

Henri Rousseau (1844–1910) was known as Le Douanier because that was his job: a customs officer. He was essentially an amateur painter, and because he was self-taught, he brought to art a completely new vision. He is famous, above all, for his imaginary jungle scenes, richly colored and deftly painted, with naive images based on pictures from popular magazines. He was not successful until late in life, when he was championed by young, radical artists such as Picasso (see pages 104–5).

POINTILLISM

The use of small dabs of paint was an important element of the Impressionist technique. In the 1880s two painters, Georges Seurat (1859–91) and Paul Signac (1863–35), took this idea one step further, composing paintings entirely from tiny dots of pure color. The dots merge when the paintings are viewed from a distance. Pointillism (or Neo-impressionism) had considerable success for a while, and the best paintings have a strangely luminous and monumental quality. Seurat died at the age of 31, but Signac went on painting in the Pointillist style well into the 20th century.

Vincent van Gogh

One of the best-known painters of the Postimpressionist era was Vincent van Gogh (1853–90), a Dutch-born artist who worked in France for the last part of his short career. Determined and energetic, Van Gogh had an original, highly expressive way of painting. In 1888 Gauguin came to visit him in Arles, in the south of France, to try to form a new art colony, but they argued and van Gogh cut off part of his own ear. In May 1889 van Gogh was admitted into a mental asylum at Saint-Rémy de Provence and stayed there for a year. That is where he painted *The Starry Night* (see below). Van Gogh sold very few of his paintings and lived in poverty. He was awkward, depressive, and misunderstood. He ended his life in 1890 by shooting himself in a field near Paris at the age of 37. Gauguin died on the South Pacific island of Hiva Oa in 1903, impoverished, lonely, sick, and frustrated by his lack of recognition.

Left: Van Gogh painted the very modest world that surrounded him, giving his possessions a charming dignity. This is his room in Arles, painted in 1888.

SHOWCASE: VINCENT VAN GOGH, *THE STARRY NIGHT*

Within a few years of their deaths, art collectors were paying high prices for works by van Gogh and Gauguin—and today their paintings are worth tens of millions of dollars. The story of both van Gogh and Gauguin helped to create a 20th-century romantic myth that great artists—by virtue of their originality—must suffer in the outer margins of society to stay true to their art.

The sky is full of huge swirling shapes, beautiful and spectacular but also unsettling, given van Gogh's state of mind.

Van Gogh was fascinated by the wiry shapes of cypress trees, a feature of the landscape of southern France.

The heavy impasto (thickly applied paint) is an indication of the feverish passion with which van Gogh worked.

A village sits quietly beneath the raging night sky. This was an imagined scene: van Gogh did not paint it outdoors.

Toulouse-Lautrec

Aristocratic by birth, Henri de Toulouse-Lautrec (1864–1901) cut a distinctive figure in the trendsetting art world of Paris, where he was a friend of many of the Impressionists and Postimpressionists. He dressed smartly, but two childhood accidents had left him with very short legs. A gifted painter and draftsman, Toulouse-Lautrec specialized in depicting the bars, cafés, theaters, circuses, racetracks, and dance halls of Paris, often relishing in their somewhat seedy aspects. He was also a master of lithography, a method of printing that allowed plenty of expression because the printing plates were made by drawing freely in wax crayon on a large stone. Toulouse-Lautrec became famous for his lithograph posters, made to advertise the music halls and dance halls. The influence of Japanese prints can be seen in his strikingly unconventional compositions.

Left: In this painting of 1890, Toulouse-Lautrec uses a typically unusual composition to depict the male dancer known as Valentin le Desossé (Boneless Valentin), seen in the mid-distance, training a female dancer at the famous cabaret the Moulin Rouge.

Official Art

Most of the public sculpture of the 19th century was commissioned and made as a kind of government propaganda, to celebrate national heroes and values. By and large it was unremarkable, but there were exceptions. François Rude (1784–1855) was a French sculptor who worked in the Romantic style, which he used to express his deeply patriotic fervor. His most famous work adorns the Arc de Triomphe in Paris, a complex piece full of vitality. Called *La Marseillaise* (1833–36), after the French national anthem, it features six warriors beneath the figure of Winged Victory.

Left: François Rude was a passionate supporter of Napoleon. His strange marble monument called Awakening to Immortality *(1846) shows Napoleon arising from the dead and casting off his shroud.*

Below left: The Statue of Liberty was shipped in sections from France to its island in New York Harbor, where it was completed in 1886.

19th-Century Sculpture

For most of the 19th century, sculpture followed the patterns of previous eras. Neoclassical sculpture remained the norm. Early in the century, a number of sculptors injected the passion of the romantic era into their work. The French sculptor Antoine-Louis Barye (1796–1875) created expressive bronze depictions of wild beasts, both real and mythical, often in anger or combat. But the century had to await the arrival of the French sculptor Auguste Rodin (1840–1917) for someone who could really ignite international attention. After studying Michelangelo's work in Italy, he caused a sensation in 1878 with an extraordinarily naturalistic naked male figure called *The Age of Bronze*.

The Statue of Liberty

One of the most famous sculptors at the time was the Frenchman Frédéric-Auguste Bartholdi (1834–1904), and his fame rested almost entirely on his greatest work: the Statue of Liberty. It was designed as a gift from France to the United States, a fellow republic, to mark the centennial of the American Declaration of Independence in 1776. Bartholdi began with a clay model 4 feet (1.2 m) high, which was then enlarged nearly 40 times to create the famous final statue, made of hollow copper.

In the United States

The United States produced a number of fine sculptors in the 19th century, many of them working in the field of public monuments. Several of them trained and worked in Italy, including perhaps the best of the American Neoclassical sculptors, William Henry Rinehart (1825–74). He produced marble busts and female nudes, and, in 1870, the charming group *Latona and Her Children* (the sleeping infant gods Apollo and Diana). Among the greatest sculptors of the next generation was Augustus Saint-Gaudens (1848–1907), who was famous for his monuments to the heroes of the Civil War (1861–65). This included impressive equestrian statues, such as the bronze monument to General Sherman (1892–1903), with Winged Victory, in New York's Central Park. His famous relief sculpture for the Robert Gould Shaw Memorial in Boston took him 14 years to complete.

Left: Augustus Saint-Gaudens's bronze Robert Gould Shaw Memorial (1884–97) celebrates one of the first all-black regiments recruited in the North to fight for the Union Army during the Civil War.

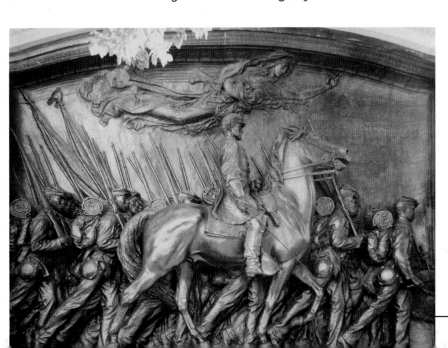

Real Bodies

Unlike classical sculptors, Rodin did not idealize the human body. His figures might be strong and fit, but they were closely based on real people: He often used acrobats and dancers as models. In fact, his figures looked so naturalistic that some people suspected him of making molds directly from live models. The figures in many of his most famous sculptures, such as *The Thinker* (1882) and *The Kiss* (1886), certainly look very real and human, but Rodin also exaggerated the human form and injected intense emotion into his sculptures—as seen in *The Burghers of Calais* (see below). Rodin's work liberated sculpture from the restrictions of the past and represents a major turning point in the history of art.

Left: Rodin's sculpture The Thinker *was one of several famous pieces that he first designed on a small scale for his monumental bronze doors called* The Gates of Hell, *for the Museum of Decorative Arts in Paris—a project he never completed.*

Materials

By and large, sculptors were working with the same traditional materials that had been used for centuries. Many of Rodin's pieces were modeled in clay or plaster and then cast in bronze, but he also worked in marble—often leaving parts of the stone with a deliberate rough and unfinished look, as Michelangelo had done. The painter Edgar Degas (see pages 92 and 94) was also a gifted sculptor, modeling delicate, small-scale pieces depicting dancers, bathers, and horses. He made these in wax and clay, and they were cast in bronze only after his death. His *Little Fourteen-Year-Old Dancer* (c. 1881) was the only sculpture that he exhibited during his lifetime.

Left: Bronze copies of Degas' Little Fourteen-Year-Old Dancer are dressed in a real cloth tutu, like the original wax version.

SHOWCASE: RODIN, *THE BURGHERS OF CALAIS*

The striking naturalism and modernity of Rodin's sculpture had great appeal in the age of Impressionism. By comparison, the traditional, academic style of classical sculpture seemed stale. Rodin was commissioned to do various major projects for public institutions. One of the most famous was his group of life-size bronze figures called *The Burghers of Calais* (1885–95), a public monument designed to stand in front of the town hall in the northern French city of Calais. It depicts six leading citizens (burghers) of Calais who, during an English siege in 1347, volunteered to sacrifice themselves to save their city. Because it lacked the heroic ideals normally found in public sculpture, it caused great controversy.

The six figures each show different reactions to the stress of the moment, believing they would be executed. (In fact, they were spared.)

Twelve sets of casts were made of each of the individual statues. Now found in various parts of the world, the group has been arranged in a variety of ways. This version is in the Hirshhorn Sculpture Garden in Washington, D.C.

According to the story, the burghers were dressed in rags and carried rope nooses.

One of the town leaders, Eustache de Saint-Pierre, has the wretched task of delivering the city's keys to the enemy.

Rodin wanted the statues in Calais to stand at ground level—unusual for public sculpture. (They were placed on a low pedestal in 1924.)

Symbolists

During the middle decades of the 19th century, modern trends in painting had been dominated by Realism. But as the century drew to a close, a number of artists (along with poets and writers) from all over Europe found themselves more attracted to the world of the imagination—to the rich and vague domain of myth, dreams, and emotion. They became known as the Symbolists because much of their work symbolized, or evoked, something beyond what was actually depicted (in contrast to the work of Realists). The label applied to a very broad variety of artists and styles: Paul Gauguin (see page 96) is sometimes also included.

Above: Vase of Flowers *(1914),* in pastel and pencil, is one of Redon's numerous pictures of flowers in vases, painted in his distinctively vibrant color range.

Odilon Redon
The dreamlike world portrayed in the works of Odilon Redon (1840–1916) includes religious and mythical figures, angels, spiders with human faces, and one-eyed monsters. He depicted these in bright colors and in startlingly eccentric compositions, and they constitute some of his most curious and original images. Even his numerous pictures of vases of flowers seem unreal, and more than what they appear to be. Much of his work expresses ideas drawn from literature admired by the Symbolists.

Gustave Moreau
The French painter Gustave Moreau (1826–98) specialized in powerful paintings on mythological and biblical themes, some of them hauntingly bizarre. These were richly painted in the academic tradition, but Moreau brought his own kind of mystery to his work through his darkly intense colors, feathery lines, and intense emotional content. Symbolism is often associated with a kind of dreamy, gloomy mood called fin de siècle (end of the century), which is said to have accompanied the final years of the 19th century. Much of Moreau's work has that feel to it. Moreau was also a notable teacher: Matisse (see pages 102–3) was one of his pupils.

Below: In Orpheus *(1865), Moreau depicts his interpretation of the Greek myth of Orpheus, poet and lyre player, whose head and lyre continue to sing mournful songs after his death.*

Above: Hammershøi's wife, Ida, was often featured in his paintings, as in this work simply called Interior *(1898).*

Vilhelm Hammershøi
The Danish artist Vilhelm Hammershøi (1864–1916) is most famous for his detailed, delicate depictions of interiors, painted in a very limited range of somber colors. They are reminiscent of the interior scenes by Vermeer (see pages 62–63), except that the rooms are usually very sparsely furnished—or completely bare, with a door opening onto other empty rooms. If there are figures, they often have their backs turned. There is a beauty in these calm, silent rooms, but they are also unsettling, like a glimpse of a sad dream. Hammershøi was born in Copenhagen and spent most of his working life there, living in an old mansion—the subject of more than 60 such interiors.

Pierre Puvis de Chavannes

Centuries of Western art are evoked in the paintings of the French artist Pierre Puvis de Chavannes (1824–98)—Giotto, Cranach, Poussin, and others. Puvis de Chavannes painted mainly mythical, biblical, and allegorical subjects. From the 1870s, he began using a distinctive color range of soft and chalky blues, greens, and whites, painted in blocks of flat color. This is because they were designed as murals, and—although they were painted in oil on canvas—he wanted them to look like Renaissance frescoes. Highly respected in his day, Puvis de Chavannes was also much admired by a number of Postimpressionists.

Left: Prometheus, *by Puvis de Chavannes, looks cheerful— but depicts a savage Greek myth. For stealing fire from the gods, Prometheus was punished by being chained to a rock, where an eagle came daily to gnaw at his liver.*

Ferdinand Hodler

In 1891 the Swiss artist Ferdinand Hodler (1853–1918) painted *The Night*, a highly controversial piece featuring naked slumbering people, except one who is awoken by the nightmarish, shrouded figure of Death. Hodler injected new invention and imagination into his work, with mysterious figures stretching right across his canvases, and sometimes lined up in oddly neat ranks. His landscapes also became increasingly simple, dominated by unusual horizontals. In 1904 he became a member of the Vienna Secession (see below).

Above: Schynige Platte *(1909) takes its name from the place where Hodler painted this view of the Jungfrau Mountain.*

SHOWCASE: KLIMT, *PORTRAIT OF ADELE BLOCH-BAUER*

The Austrian artist Gustav Klimt (1862–1918) was a dynamic painter, decorator, and teacher, and a leader of the radical art and design movement called the Vienna Secession. He had the skills of a technical painter in the academic tradition, but he also had a Symbolist's eye for the weird and mysterious, and he liked to fill his paintings with a rich mass of highly inventive decoration. He worked on this portrait of Adele Bloch-Bauer, the wife of a wealthy industrialist, over a period of three years (1904–7).

The face occupies only a small proportion of the total surface area. The rest is decoration.

The face and hands have some of the exaggeration that Klimt often used when depicting the human body.

Adele Bloch-Bauer wears lavish jewelry, but the whole painting is like a giant piece of jewelry.

The textiles of the dress and high-back chair merge into one, a virtually abstract quilt of swirls, geometric shapes, and eyelike motifs.

The gold is made of real gold leaf.

Nabis and Fauves

In 1888 a group of French painters in Paris formed a secretive group called the Nabis ("prophets" in Hebrew) to devise a new approach to art. Led by Paul Sérusier, they included Pierre Bonnard, Édouard Vuillard, and Maurice Denis (1870–1943); they stayed together as a group until about 1900. It was Denis who perhaps best summarized their aim: "Remember that a picture, before being a warhorse, a nude or some kind of story, is essentially a flat surface covered with colors arranged in a certain order." In 1901 Henri Matisse, Maurice de Vlaminck, and André Derain began painting in another revolutionary way, using masses of bright color freely applied. When they exhibited their work in the 1905 Salon d'Automne, a critic declared they were like *fauves* (wild beasts).

Above: Vuillard's Woman in Blue with a Child *(c. 1899) is essentially a composition of shapes and colors made busy with the patterning of the bed cover and wallpaper.*

Édouard Vuillard

In the early days of Nabi painting, Édouard Vuillard (1868–1940) used a combination of flat areas of color and impressionist dots to build up his compositions—usually depicting rather charming scenes of contemporary family life. He shared a studio with Bonnard, and together they explored the possibilities of surface pattern. Their work had many similarities: Perspective is often distorted, with compositions off-center and cut off by the frame. Over time, their paintings became richer in color and more complex.

Paul Sérusier

The Nabis were fascinated by a painting by Paul Sérusier (1864–1927) called *L'Aven au Bois d'Amour* (*The River Aven at the Wood of Love*), painted in 1888. Thinking that this painting somehow pointed to the future of art, the Nabis renamed it *The Talisman*. Sérusier had worked in Brittany alongside Paul Gauguin (see page 96) and was inspired by Gauguin's use of blocks of color. *The Talisman* effectively took this idea to the next logical stage. Sérusier's other work was more figurative, and he later painted religious subjects, but still showed his love of shapes and flat color.

Below: The Nabis experimented with the shape of paintings. Bonnard's Nannies out for a Walk, with Frieze of Hackney Carriages *(1895) is a four-panel screen made from a lithograph print.*

Above: Sérusier's small landscape painting L'Aven au Bois d'Amour *(The* Talisman*) (1888) had a special place in the Nabis' theory of art.*

Pierre Bonnard

Like Vuillard, Pierre Bonnard (1867–1947) was highly experimental in his Nabi years, playing with flat shapes and surfaces, and much influenced by the composition of Japanese prints. After 1900 he developed a distinctive technique of strong shapes and rich, joyful color, often applied in short and bold brushstrokes. He painted landscapes, figures, and portraits, and, above all, interiors filled with light—but he was always concerned with the way that the composition worked across the entire surface of the painting.

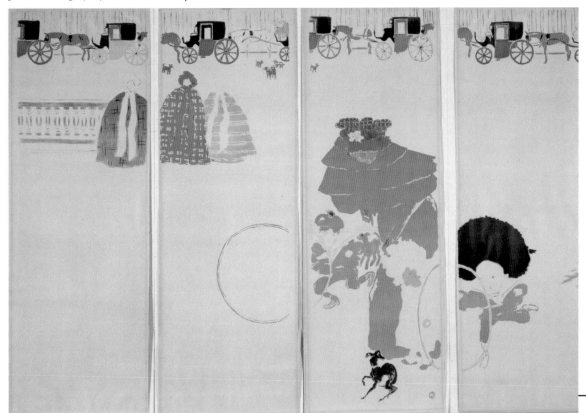

*Left: Like all Fauvist painting,
Vlaminck's* Red Trees *(1906) is an
expression of feeling rather than
an accurate visual record.*

Maurice de Vlaminck

Born in France to Flemish parents, Maurice de Vlaminck
(1876–1958) began his career as a racing cyclist and violinist,
painting as a hobby. He was proud of the fact that he had no
formal art training—and claimed that he had never set foot in
Paris's greatest gallery of historical art, the Louvre. However, in
1901 he was inspired by an exhibition of paintings by van Gogh
(see page 97). This is when he also met Matisse, and he went with
Matisse and André Derain (1880–1954) to Collioure, a Mediterranean
fishing village in southwest France, in the summer of 1905.
There they produced many of the paintings that would shock the
critics at the Salon d'Automne later that year. Vlaminck continued
to paint in the Fauvist style, more or less, for his entire career.

SHOWCASE: MATISSE, *THE RED STUDIO*

Henri Matisse (1869–1954) was one of the
outstanding painters of the 20th century.
He rocketed to the forefront of the Paris art scene
in 1905 as the leader of the Fauves, and Fauvism
became the dominant trend until about 1908.
After this, Matisse continued to experiment with
color and form until his death at the age of 84.
The Red Studio (1911) dates from a period when
Matisse was testing the extreme possibilities of
using flat areas of color. The painting depicts
Matisse's own studio in Issy-les-Moulineaux,
a suburb of Paris.

At the center is a grandfather clock,
without hands—suggesting that time
is meaningless in his studio.

The studio was actually white, but Matisse
believed that this shade of red was the only
color that could bring a satisfactory unity
to the other elements of the composition.

The studio contains his own recent
paintings and ceramics. These are
virtually the only items picked out in
color from the red background.

Most of the furniture is depicted only
in outline (scraped through the red
paint). Matisse's prime interest was to
create a satisfactory arrangement of
shapes and colors.

Georges Braque

Like many young painters in Paris, Georges Braque (1882–1963) was converted to
fauvism in 1905, largely through his friendship with another Fauvist painter, Raoul Dufy
(1877–1953). He painted in this style for about two years. He was particularly drawn to
harbor scenes, depicting them in a fairly naturalistic way in terms of composition but
placing bold emphasis on the shapes of the boats and elements of the landscape, and
flooding the whole painting with lively color. In 1907, however, Braque met Picasso, and
together they worked on the next great trend in Western art: Cubism (see page 104).
Braque remained a confirmed Cubist for the rest of his life and tended to underplay his
earlier experimentation with Fauvism—but Fauvism clearly was an important stepping
stone in his development as an artist.

Left: Braque painted The Harbor
at Antwerp *in 1906, in the middle
of his Fauvist phase.*

CUBISM

Picasso was fascinated by the work of Paul Cézanne (see page 95), who spent most of his painting career seeing how he could break pictures of landscapes and still lifes into geometric forms. Picasso and his colleague Georges Braque (see page 103) took this one radical step further. They broke up the visual world into flat, rectangular surfaces and also looked at what might happen if they tried to paint objects and people from various angles in the same picture. Cubism was launched in 1908. The first phase is known as analytical Cubism, because they analyzed the visual world. But after 1912 they began to take a looser, more playful approach, using brighter colors, simpler forms, and collage; this was known as Synthetic Cubism. Picasso's cubist period lasted until World War I (1914-18), a depressing and sobering time for Europe, which forced him to rethink his approach to art.

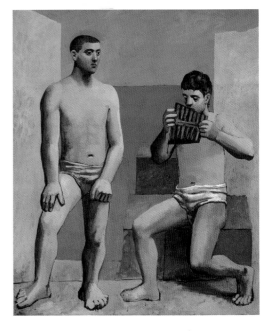

Above: In The Pipes of Pan *(1923) Picasso applied a modern approach to a classical theme.*

Left: Picasso gave the Cubist treatment to his Portrait of Ambroise Vollard *(1910), a portrait of a celebrated art dealer. The visual world had never been painted quite like this before.*

Below: Three Musicians (1921) is actually an oil painting, but Picasso is playing a visual joke: It looks like a collage of paper cutouts.

Inspiration

Picasso took his inspiration from a wide range of art. He studied the great painters of the past, as well as the Postimpressionists and more recent trendsetters. He was also fascinated by African and other non-European art and sculpture, and was one of the first modern artists to show this influence in his work. All the while he was exploring new ways to reappraise and interpret the visual world, often taking leaps of imagination into completely new territory. The work illustrated on these two pages shows the immense variety of his painting styles.

Picasso

Pablo Picasso (1881–1973) was the single greatest artist of the 20th century. A technically gifted draftsman, he showed unusual talent as a child in his homeland of Spain. In 1900 he went to Paris—still the world's art capital—to seek fame and fortune, and settled there permanently in 1904. Initially he worked on moody figurative paintings in his blue period (1901–4) and his rose period (1904–6). Envious of the success of Matisse as the leader of the Fauves, Picasso developed a completely new theory of art: Cubism. This became hugely influential, but Picasso never stuck to one style for long: He was constantly exploring new directions for painting and sculpture. In fact, Picasso was so inventive and industrious that over his long life he produced a range of work that at least six other artists might have done, and each become famous for.

Collage

As a hobby, the Victorians had amused themselves by cutting out printed images and scraps of cloth and sticking them down to make pictures. No one thought that this was a technique suitable for fine art. So when Picasso and Braque began sticking bits of wallpaper, newspaper clippings, and pieces of printed musical scores into their Cubist paintings, this was a radical departure. Picasso also stuck larger "found objects" onto his paintings, such as pieces of wood and spoons, making them three-dimensional—part painting, part sculpture.

Portraits

Picasso painted numerous portraits throughout his career. They range hugely, from the Cubist work, as seen in his *Portrait of Ambroise Vollard*, to wildly imaginative and stylized images, as seen in *The Red Armchair*. There is a clear progression between the two: Picasso was experimenting with the limits to which he could push the conventions of figure drawing. Many of his portraits are of women, and unnamed, but they often depict his wives or lovers. He tended to change his style every time the woman in his life changed. He painted his first wife, Olga, in an almost conventional portrait in 1917; *The Red Armchair* dates from the period after he had met his new love, Marie-Thérèse Walter.

Left: The Red Armchair *(1931) shows how a woman's face might be painted looking straight ahead and to the side at the same time, or as if turning her head.*

Left: Picasso's distinctive signature became well known in his lifetime, and its presence on any drawing or print markedly increased its value.

Below: By putting together a bicycle seat and handlebars, Picasso made a sculpture on one of his favorite themes. His playful Head of a Bull *(1943) was later cast in bronze.*

Sculpture

Picasso was an extraordinarily inventive sculptor and took sculpture into completely new directions. He liked to incorporate "found objects": For instance, a toy car suggested a baboon's head to him, so he used it to make *Baboon and Young* (1951), cast in bronze. *Goat* (1950) was made from a wicker basket, ceramic pots, palm leaves, and pieces of wood and metal. Picasso used welded metal rods and flat sheets of metal to create sculptures of human figures and heads. He made sculptures out of cardboard. And in the 1940s, when he lived in the south of France, he took up pottery, decorating plates and bowls with extravagant designs.

SHOWCASE: PICASSO, *GUERNICA*

While Picasso lived in France, his homeland was torn apart by the Spanish Civil War (1936–39), fought between the Republicans and the Fascists. In a gruesome incident in 1937, the Basque town of Guernica was bombed from the air by the Germans, who were allies of the Spanish fascists; many innocent people were killed. Shortly afterward Picasso began work on a commission for the Republican government of Spain to paint a mural for the Spanish pavilion at the 1937 International Exposition in Paris. He chose the bombing of Guernica as his subject, and completed this huge black-and-white painting in just three weeks. It is one of the most powerful comments in the history of art on the senseless savagery of war.

A woman holding her dead child wails in anguish.

The bull links up with Picasso's interest in the mythology of the Minotaur, and the Spanish tradition of bullfighting. He saw it as a symbol of brutality and darkness.

All life suffers in war, including a horse wounded by a spear.

A woman holds out a lamp, shedding light—perhaps the light of truth—on the tangle of limbs and the pain and suffering.

A flower (symbol of peace) grows from the sword held by the severed arms of the fallen warrior.

Fire engulfs a screaming woman.

Expressionism

While the Fauves filled their canvases with expressive, non-naturalistic color in France, in 1905 a parallel group formed in Dresden, Germany, called Die Brücke (The Bridge). What united them was their desire to paint primarily about emotion—sometimes restrained and meditative, but often raw and angry—usually by distorting reality in some way. This was nothing new: Such expressive distortion could be found in the 15th-century paintings of Rogier van der Weyden (see page 48) and, more recently, in the work of Vincent van Gogh (see page 97). But now it had a name: Expressionism.

Above: Schiele's Portrait of Paul Erdmann in a Sailor Suit *(c. 1913) catches his nephew looking lonely and unhappy.*

Oskar Kokoschka

The term *expressionist* had been used in the late 19th-centruy, but the concept of Expressionism as a distinct movement in art and literature was promoted by a German magazine devoted to it, *Der Sturm* (*The Storm*), founded in 1910. The Austrian artist Oskar Kokoschka (1886–1980) contributed artwork to *Der Sturm* in the years leading up to World War I. Kokoschka's painting was passionate and highly energized, often showing distorted bodies painted with vigorous brushstokes. But he could also adapt this style to produce penetrating portraits. Kokoschka was severely wounded in the war. He spent the following years teaching and traveling, and still painting in an Expressionist style, but with a brighter color range. Like many artists in Germany and Austria, he had to flee the Nazis in the 1930s, and he settled in Switzerland after World War II.

Egon Schiele

Expressionism could be expressed in color, or simply in the way in which an artist attacked the canvas with paint. In the work of some expressionist painters, however, the emotion is more delicately and subtly implied, but it lies beneath the surface like a coiled spring. The Austrian artist Egon Schiele (1890–1918) was a draftsman of extraordinary power and vision. His paintings usually focus on one or two people drawn with exaggeratedly bony, contorted bodies, and often taut with emotion. A friend and protégé of Gustav Klimt (see page 101), Schiele could have become a major figure in 20th-century art if his life had not been cut short at the age of 28 by the flu epidemic of 1918.

Above: Kokoschka used Expressionist distortion in his Portrait of Karl Kraus *(1925), capturing the intellectual passion of this Austrian writer and journalist.*

Max Beckmann

Europe went through a chaotic period of history in the first half of the 20th century, with World War I, then the rise of Nazi Germany leading to World War II. The German artist Max Beckmann (1884–1950) had a traumatic experience as a medical orderly in World War I and thereafter painted highly distorted work of violent intensity about war and the sickness of modern society. His work has similarities to the more political paintings and caricatures by fellow German artists Otto Dix (1891–1969) and George Grosz (1893–1959), whose work was given the label Neue Sachlichkeit (New Objectivity). This implied that they viewed the world with an open mind and without prejudice; in fact, much of their work was savagely critical. The Nazis hated it, and both Beckmann and Grosz had to flee Germany in the 1930s.

Right: Max Beckmann had a studio in Paris and was invited to paint Paris Society *(1931) by the German embassy. Its somber, tense atmosphere seems to echo the troubled times.*

Above: Masks Confronting Death *(1888) combines all the unique characteristics of James Ensor's painting—it is bold, bizarre, humorous, and macabre.*

James Ensor

Another remarkable painter who prefigured German Expressionism was James Ensor (1860–1949), a Belgian with a British father. He began painting in an Impressionist style, but after 1883 he started producing peculiar imaginary images of masked figures, skeletons, and disturbing carnival scenes, using thick, brightly colored paint and a deliberately crude style. Such work was highly unusual at the time, and Ensor led a reclusive, somewhat eccentric life in Ostend. However, he was also closely involved in the art scene in Brussels, which was one of the most dynamic and open-minded in Europe.

Above: Marc used a distinctive, radiant, and totally unnatural range of colors for his animal paintings, as in Blue Horse II *(1911).*

Franz Marc

The painter Franz Marc (1880–1916) was one of the founders of Der Blaue Reiter (The Blue Rider), a second group of German Expressionist artists, which formed in Munich in 1912. Influences of Gauguin, Fauvism, and Cubism can be detected in Marc's poetic and spiritual form of Expressionism. Animals—and especially horses—are often the subject of his painting, reflecting his deeply religious views about the imperfections of mankind. He was killed while riding a horse at the Battle of Verdun in 1916.

SHOWCASE: MUNCH, *RED VIRGINIA CREEPER*

An early pioneer of Expressionism was the Norwegian painter Edvard Munch (1863–1944). His most famous painting, *The Scream* (1893), shows a figure with a skull-like, screaming head in a swirling landscape that seems to contribute, inescapably, to this mental anguish. The whole painting is emotional and deeply unsettling, and reflects Munch's own fragile state of mind. *Red Virginia Creeper*, named after the kind of ivy growing all over the house depicted, was painted in 1898–1900, when Munch was living mainly in Berlin. Essentially, it depicts an utterly ordinary scene, yet in Munch's hands it is feverish with stress.

The creeper seems to be choking the house; its stems look like veins, and its leaves like blood.

The perspective of the house, and the blank windows, make it look menacing, as if some tragedy has taken place here.

The figure in the foreground has a dazed expression, as though walking away from something that haunts him.

The curving ruts in the road link the man to the house. Cover them over to see the role they play in giving the picture its sense of emotional anguish.

The First
Abstract
Artists

There is much dispute about who was the first abstract artist. In 1910 Wassily Kandinsky (1866–1944), a founder of the German expressionist group Der Blaue Reiter (see page 107), began a series of paintings containing only colors and shapes, and not representing anything in the real world. That is, essentially, the definition of abstract art. Others were doing the same thing at about the same time, including the American Arthur Dove (1880–1946). This was a complete break with the past. Prior to this, the history of art had been about finding ways to represent the world as we see it. In the early years, however, many artists still took ideas from the visual world as a starting point for semiabstract interpretations of them.

Below: Amorpha *means "shapeless," and a fugue is a type of musical composition. Kupka's intentions are clear in this study for his* Amorpha, Fugue in Two Colors *(1912).*

Above: In Composition No. II (Composition en Rouge, Bleu et Jaune, 1930), *Mondrian has reduced painting to rectangular shapes with primary colors. The art is in the balance of the composition.*

De Stijl

In 1912 the Dutch artist Piet Mondrian (1872–1944) was in Paris when he began a famous series of Cubist-style paintings of apple trees. Gradually they became more and more abstract. In 1914 he returned to the Netherlands and developed a style of painting based entirely on horizontal and vertical lines and rectangles filled with color. Mondrian became a founder of a movement of artists and designers based on this work. It was called, simply, De Stijl, meaning "The Style." He continued working on this theme for the rest of his life, living in Paris, then London, and finally New York.

Orphism

In 1911, when analytical Cubism (see page 104) still had a predominantly somber tone, a group of artists in Paris tried to inject more color into their Cubist-inspired work, along with a greater sense of poetry. They included the French painter Robert Delaunay (1885–1941) and the Czech-born painter Frantisek Kupka (1871–1957). They also wanted to show how Cubism related to music, and so they adopted the label Orphic cubism, after Orpheus, the lyre player in Greek mythology (see page 100). The Orphist experiment soon led to completely abstract painting, usually based on sweeping curves and blocks of bright but textured color. As a movement, Orphism lasted only until World War I, but it had a major impact on the development of modern art.

Suprematism

In Moscow in 1915 the Russian artist Kasimir Malevich (1878–1935) exhibited the most extreme abstract painting yet: a black square on a white background. Malevich wanted to create a movement of radical abstract art. He called it Suprematism because he believed that, in art, artistic sensitivity alone was supreme and was all that mattered. His other work at this time contained only rectangles of color laid onto a white or pale background. In 1918 he made a series of paintings with a white square painted onto a white background. After this, he felt that Suprematism had run its course, and later returned to figurative painting.

Above: Malevich usually gave no indication about what his abstract painting referred to. Suprematist Composition: Airplane Flying *(1914–15) is an exception.*

Above: Duchamp's Nude Descending a Staircase *(1912) combined Cubism with the kind of stop-motion technique used by the Futurists to indicate movement.*

Marcel Duchamp

The French artist Marcel Duchamp (1887–1968) shot to fame and notoriety at the Armory Show in New York in 1913 with his *Nude Descending a Staircase*. After this he painted very little, but instead produced sculptural pieces, called ready-mades, from objects he had found. By stating that art is essentially about selection (rather than technique), he laid the foundations for many of the later developments in art in the 20th century.

Right: In Swifts: Paths of Movement + Dynamic Sequences *(1913) Balla takes the flight of birds as his starting point for a study of motion and speed.*

Giacomo Balla

Yet another new art movement, called Futurism, was launched in 1909. This involved mainly Italian painters, including Giacomo Balla (1871–1958). They enthused about the wonders of the modern world—the age of the machine, speed, cities, and factories. To illustrate the frenetic motion of this world, Balla used multiple overlaid images, and gradually his work became more fragmented and increasingly abstract. By 1913 he was producing a series of paintings with titles such as *Abstract Speed + Sound*.

SHOWCASE: KANDINSKY, *STUDY FOR COMPOSITION II*

From about 1909, Wassily Kandinsky gradually edged toward abstract painting. One night, he said, he went into his studio, saw one of his paintings standing upside down, and was struck by its beauty—and this was the moment when he realized the potential of painting that did not represent anything. *Composition II* was painted at about this time, but it is not a fully abstract painting. The imagery relates to his recurring theme of a rider on horseback—which gave rise to the name of his Expressionist group, Der Blaue Reiter (The Blue Rider). Here we see a sketch (painted in oil on canvas) made in preparation of the final piece.

At the center of the painting is a white horse being ridden by a rider in blue. This could signify one of the mythical horsemen of the apocalypse, who brings massive destruction to the world.

On the right of the painting are scenes of destruction: Bodies lie strewn on the ground.

On the left is paradise, which follows the destruction wrought by the horseman.

Seven Wonders of
Modern Architecture

Over the last 200 years or so, the changing styles of architecture have gone hand in hand with the development of building materials. Advances in the manufacture of steel, concrete, and glass have allowed architects not only to design ever higher buildings, but also to use materials in a more sculptural way. In the course of the 19th century, architects felt they had to liberate themselves from the styles of the past, and they broke away from the classical model originally established by the ancient Greeks—although it has never been fully abandoned. In the 20th century, they felt bold enough to build in any shape or form they fancied. Nonetheless, there are always practical constraints.

Above: The famous clock tower known as Big Ben stands over the Houses of Parliament at the Palace of Westminster, London.

Sagrada Familia

The Church of the Sagrada Familia (Sacred Family) in Barcelona, Spain, is one of the world's most extraordinary buildings. Started in 1879, it is the most famous work of Antoní Gaudí (1852–1926). Gaudí worked in a style called Art Nouveau (new art), which was all the rage in Europe from about 1890 to 1914. The intention with Art Nouveau was to establish a completely fresh approach to design that was free of any reference to past styles. This is certainly the case with the Sagrada Familia—but its construction proved so challenging that it is still not finished.

Right: The concrete front of the Sagrada Familia was inspired by dribbled sand and the spires by maize husks.

Below: The Sydney Opera House has a spectacular location on the edge of Sydney Harbor and beside the Sydney Harbor Bridge.

The Houses of Parliament

In 1834 the old Houses of Parliament in London were destroyed in a fire (see page 85). They were rebuilt in a style called Gothic revival, based on the medieval Gothic style (see pages 34–35)—very different from the Neoclassical style in which most public buildings were then being built. This was a deliberate choice because the Neoclassical style had been used for the White House and Congress in the United States, and Britain did not wish to be reminded of American independence. The Gothic design by Charles Barry (1795–1860) was selected from among 97 rival bids; building began in 1840 and was completed in 1852.

The Eiffel Tower

In just two years, starting in 1887, the world's tallest structure, built entirely of iron, rose above the streets of Paris—a marvel of the age. The Eiffel Tower was the centerpiece of the 1889 Universal Exposition, a huge international fair to mark the centennial of the French Revolution. It is named after its designer, the French engineer Alexandre-Gustave Eiffel (1832–1923).

Left: Rising to the height of an 80-story building, the instantly recognizable, curving shape of the Eiffel Tower remains the symbol of Paris to this day.

Sydney Opera House

All cities want a symbol that the world will remember them by. Sydney, Australia's largest city, achieved this with its opera house. The distinctive cluster of giant, shell-like roofs was designed by the Danish architect Jørn Utzon (born 1918), who submitted sketches to a competition in 1955. Construction proved more difficult and more costly than expected, and Utzon resigned from the project in 1966. The engineering problems were eventually solved, however, and the Sydney Opera House finally opened in 1973.

Notre Dame du Haut

Charles-Édouard Jeanneret-Gris (1887–1965), a Swiss-born French architect, is better known by his professional name: Le Corbusier. He came to international attention at the 1925 International Exposition of Modern Decorative and Industrial Arts, in Paris, for which he designed an ultramodern, all-white, cubelike dwelling. It was a foretaste of what was later called the modernist movement. Le Corbusier became known for his radically functional designs, using concrete and plate glass and cutting out all decorative trimmings. But Notre Dame du Haut is an exception. Completed in 1955, it is a hilltop pilgrimage chapel at Ronchamp, in southeastern France. With barely a right angle in sight, and with its dramatically curving roof of rough-cast concrete inspired by the shell of a crab, it is far more sculptural than Le Corbusier's other work, and it is much admired for its sense of profound spirituality.

Below: The thick walls of Notre Dame du Haut are pierced by small windows of plain and colored glass, seemingly in random order, allowing natural light to filter into the dark, tranquil interior.

The Skyscraper

The term *skyscraper* was first applied to buildings in the United States in the 1890s. For more than a decade, office blocks had been growing taller and taller. This had been made possible by the development of iron-framed buildings: The iron skeleton took all the weight, and the walls became simply "curtains." If the walls had taken the weight, it would have been possible to build only to a height of about five stories. Another crucial factor was the invention of the elevator—first developed by Elisha Otis in New York in 1857. Without this, high-rise buildings would have been impractical. New York became the greatest skyscraper city as major American companies competed with each other to build headquarters in ever higher and more elaborate tower blocks. The Chrysler automobile company chose the fashionable Art Deco style for its headquarters, designed by William van Alen (1883–1953).

Below left: Completed in 1929, the Chrysler Building overtook the Eiffel Tower as the world's tallest structure, but the Empire State Building quickly surpassed it in 1930.

SHOWCASE: FRANK LLOYD WRIGHT, THE GUGGENHEIM MUSEUM, NEW YORK

One of the most celebrated modern American architects, Frank Lloyd Wright (1867–1959) worked as a young man with Louis Henry Sullivan (1856–1924), pioneer of the skyscraper, who had a strong belief that the function of a building should dictate how it looks. Function plays a key role in all of Wright's buildings, but so too does nature, which, he believed, has an essential healing power. The Solomon R. Guggenheim Museum, a modern art museum in New York, was one of Wright's last projects, completed in 1959.

Natural light floods in through the glass ceiling that spans the central atrium.

The paintings are displayed on the walls of the ramps and in adjacent rooms. The permanent collection includes work by Picasso, Braque, Kandinsky, Mondrian, and Modigliani, among many others.

Inside, a ramp spirals down through the levels. The design has been compared to a white snail shell.

The exterior looks like a series of white ribbons of concrete, in a cone shape, tapering toward the bottom. In 1959 this was a revolutionary shape for a building.

Salvador Dalí

The most famous of all the Surrealists was the Spanish painter Salvador Dalí (1904–89). This is partly because he was such a good self-publicist. His life was as surreal as his art—he was regularly in the news because of his madcap antics. His work was widely reproduced as prints and posters, and so his most famous paintings are familiar around the world. Dalí is best known for his strange desert landscapes, painted with great precision and featuring a mixture of bizarre elements, such as elephants on stilts, burning giraffes, female nudes, fingers made of rock, and peculiar blobs that seem to be part rock, part flesh. He also made a celebrated Surrealist film with the Spanish director Luis Buñuel, called *An Andalusian Dog* (1929). Dalí lived in the United States from 1940 to 1948, then returned to Spain where he ended his life as an eccentric recluse in Figueres, in Catalonia.

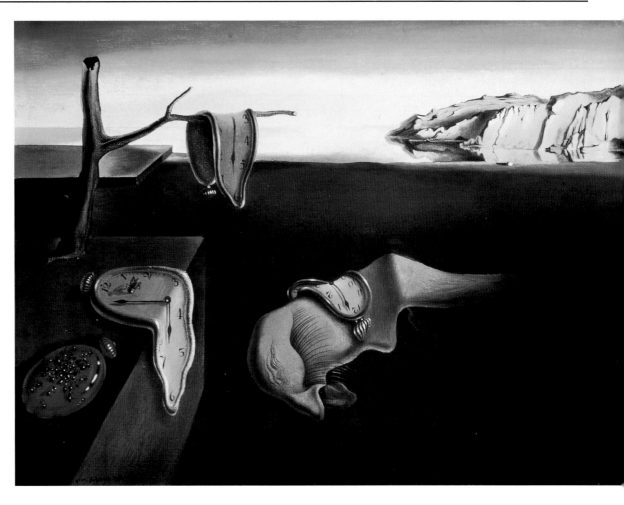

Right: The Persistence of Memory *(1931) is made weird by the melting watches, one of Dalí's best-known motifs, which calls into question the whole notion of time.*

Surrealism

During World War I, a short-lived art movement developed in neutral Switzerland that deliberately poked fun at all the traditions of art, and the world in general. It was called Dada, a nonsensical name, and its members gave madcap performances in gibberish and made throw-away art out of found objects and collage. In 1924 the French poet André Breton (1896–1966) launched a new movement called Surrealism. Like Dada, it took a sideways view of the world and promoted wacky behavior, but it had a more positive and constructive message; many of the dadaists joined it. Surrealism means "above realism": It suggested that the subconscious mind—not rational thought—held the key to the truth about the real world. The Surrealists created images that explored the realms of the subconscious—animal instinct, free association of thought, and dreams.

Giorgio de Chirico

The work of the Greek-born Italian artist Giorgio de Chirico (1888–1978) shared many of the qualities of Surrealism. He painted strangely empty streets, landscapes and interiors, and compositions with odd bits of classical sculpture and Cubist-like figures—full of eerie calm and a disturbing sense of unease. He also used a distinctive palette of drained colors. Born in Greece, De Chirico trained in Athens, Florence, and Munich, and lived in Paris from 1911 to 1915. His most famous paintings were done before the 1920s and were much admired by the Surrealists, but he never associated himself with their movement. Instead, he called his work "metaphysical painting"—meaning that it dealt with the fundamental questions of being and knowledge. When De Chirico began to paint in a more traditional style, the Surrealists criticized his work, which infuriated him, causing him to disown the earlier work that they admired.

Above: De Chirico presents a haunting, dreamlike world in The Mystery and Melancholy of a Street *(1914), made menacing by the shadow at the top.*

Above: Dutch Interior *(1928) was inspired by the paintings of the Dutch masters (see pages 62–63) that Miró saw on a visit to the Netherlands.*

Joan Miró

The work of the Spanish artist Joan Miró (1893–1983) is quite unlike the paintings normally associated with surrealism: His paintings are more like highly personalized doodles—but then doodles are often the product of the subconscious mind. They do not fit easily into any category: They are part figurative (perhaps recalling forms of microscopic animal life) and part abstract. Miró was born and trained in Barcelona but went to Paris in 1919 where he met Fauvists and Dadaists and became a close friend of fellow Spaniard Picasso. He joined the Surrealist movement in 1924. Miró claimed that he painted simply by taking up his brush, starting to create shapes, and seeing what happened. André Breton claimed that he was "the most Surrealist of all."

SHOWCASE: KLEE, *AROUND THE FISH*

The German-Swiss painter Paul Klee (1879–1940) was a member of the German Expressionist group Der Blaue Reiter (see pages 106–7). He developed his own style of small-scale painting full of quiet, meditative calm, often verging on the abstract—as though depicting his private thoughts. *Around the Fish* (1926) appears at first glance to be one of his more figurative compositions, until you look at the mysterious objects that surround the fish. Klee loved playing with symbols—here he seems to be using Christian symbols. But Klee's work generally was the product of the free association of ideas, rather than a desire to convey hidden symbolic meaning.

The five red dots could represent the five wounds of Christ on the cross. The star shape is reminiscent of the Star of David.

The die could represent the dice game played by the Roman soldiers to win Christ's garments at the Crucifixion.

The fish is a Christian symbol (from the Greek word *ichthus*, meaning "fish," which also stood for "Jesus Christ God's Son Savior" when written in Greek).

The cross is clearly a symbol of Christ's crucifixion.

The scythe is a traditional symbol of death.

René Magritte

The Belgian painter René Magritte (1898–1967) produced many of the most memorable images of Surrealism. He lived in Paris during the 1920s, when Surrealism was launched, and then returned to Brussels, where he spent the rest of his life quietly producing his meticulous, small-scale paintings in a studio at the bottom of his garden. His work is full of dreamlike absurdities, with ordinary people and objects placed in a bizarre context. Bowler-hatted businessmen rain down from the sky; a steam engine emerges from a fireplace; there are paintings within paintings; rock formations that are birds; an empty pair of boots that have real toes emerging from them. Some of Magritte's work is based on a play on words—a subconscious association that can also trigger a change of course in dreams. A picture of a tobacco pipe states in writing, "This is not a pipe"—which it is, and of course isn't.

Left: Magritte's Personal Values *(1952) contains a variety of ordinary domestic objects in a room, but their scale is absurd, and the walls dissolve into sky.*

Edward Hopper
The paintings of Edward Hopper (1882–1967) are like a record of city life in America in the first half of the 20th century. Most of his scenes take place in darkened rooms strongly lit from the side; some meeting or event may be taking place—rather like a scene from a black-and-white thriller movie of the 1930s. Some of his paintings also have an undercurrent of threat or tension; others depict a mood of loneliness or boredom. Hopper's style is distinctive and instantly recognizable: He uses large areas of flat color, and the figures are depicted deftly with rapid brushstrokes. Colors are limited and somber. Hopper presents a gritty kind of urban realism—a realism that is uniquely American, and from the America of his times.

Above: In Nighthawks *(1942), Hopper suggests the loneliness of the city, with three late-night customers lost in their private thoughts in a bar on an empty street.*

Above: Andrew Wyeth's famous painting Christina's World *(1948) suggests loneliness and frustration in the tranquil beauty of rural America. The woman depicted in fact suffered from paralysis of the lower body.*

Rural America
Building on the traditions of high-quality Realist painting established by American artists such as Thomas Eakins (see page 86), the United States produced a number of notable figurative painters in the 20th century. Grant Wood (1891–1942), a painter who worked mainly in Iowa, was influenced by Flemish artists such as Jan van Eyck (see page 49). He painted landscapes and portraits in a deliberately solid, slightly naive style. His most famous work is a painting of a farmer and his wife called *American Gothic* (1930).
Andrew Wyeth is one of the best-known and most popular American realist painters of the 20th century. He depicts the land and inhabitants around his hometown of Chadds Ford, Pennsylvania, and his summer home in Cushing, Maine. Often in his work there is an unusual, sometimes unsettling relationship between his figures and their landscape; this implies a story, which adds an intriguing note of mystery to the paintings.

The Figure
in 20th-Century Painting

Cubism and abstract art may have dislodged traditional figurative painting from the forefront of modern trends in art, but these trends did not affect all artists. Nor, indeed, did they much impress the general public, whose taste in art remained traditional—and this also included many of the people who bought paintings and provided a living for artists. There was, therefore, always a role for figurative painters. Some experimented with figurative painting, injecting it with elements drawn from other contemporary movements—such as Expressionism in the case of Francis Bacon. Others continued to paint in traditional, technically polished style. This included the American painter Andrew Wyeth (born 1917). Despite the long history of figurative painting, painters such as Amedeo Modigliani and Edward Hopper demonstrated that there was still room for new ways to convey a distinctive personal vision of the world.

Above: Pietro Annigoni (1910–88) was an Italian portrait artist who acquired international fame, largely through his famous portrait of Queen Elizabeth II (created 1954–55). He also made portraits of President John F. Kennedy and Pope John XXIII. This is a self-portrait, painted in 1946.

Left: Francis Bacon produced this striking image, simply titled Painting, in 1946, just after the end of World War II. It depicts some kind of establishment figure, half hidden under an umbrella, who seems to be responsible for the butchery that surrounds him.

Francis Bacon

The British artist Francis Bacon (1909–92) is famous for the extraordinary, tortured savagery that he brought to figurative painting. His backgrounds are often flat and plain, but in front of these his figures rave and scream. The sweeping brushstrokes of dripping paint suggest that Bacon himself felt the wild emotions expressed in the paintings. His series of paintings based on the portrait of Pope Innocent X by Velázquez (see pages 60–61), produced in the early 1950s, show a screaming figure, as if in a maddened frenzy brought on by power and corruption. In other paintings, Bacon breaks up the human face into cubist-like blocks of color, as if portraying an inner, tortured character. He also painted strange hybrid creatures, half human, half beast. Almost all of Bacon's work focuses on the pain, brutality, and ugliness of human life—and it was always shocking to the public.

Modigliani

The Italian Amedeo Modigliani (1884–1920) became widely known for his distinctive images of women. The shapes are bold, often showing a strong outline, the colors soft and grainy. But most distinctive of all are the faces—oval, simplified, and somewhat masklike (often the eyes are completely black, like the holes in a mask). Modigliani moved to Paris in 1906 and spent most of his working life there; from 1909 to 1914 he devoted himself to sculpture, inspired by the work of Constantin Brancusi (see page 117). The simplification of form that he used in his sculpture can be seen in his paintings, which were mostly completed in the last five years of his short life; he died from tuberculosis at the age of 35. Modigliani was one of several foreign figurative painters who were working in Paris at the end of World War I and who became known as the School of Paris. Others included Marc Chagall (1887–1985), a Russian from Belarus; Tsuguharu Foujita (1886–1968), from Japan; and Chaim Soutine (1893–1943), from Lithuania.

Left: With their masklike oval faces, as in Gypsy Woman with a Baby (1919), Modigliani's portraits are more a study of forms than an attempt to convey character.

SHOWCASE: GORKY, *THE ARTIST AND HIS MOTHER*

Many artists worked in several styles, both figurative and abstract, in the course of their careers, and sometimes at the same time. The American painter Arshile Gorky (1904–48) spent nearly a decade on *The Artist and His Mother* (1926–36). During these years he was also exploring Abstract Cubism. He later became known for his Surrealist painting in the style of Miró (see page 113) and was a pioneer of Abstract Expressionism (see page 118–19).

The painting was based on a photograph taken prior to his mother's death in Armenia during the Armenian genocide (1915–18); Gorky was still a boy when the photo was taken.

The dark window helps to frame the head of the mother and draw attention to her. The boy stands outside that frame.

The boy stands apart from his mother, as if to show his separation from her.

The areas of flat color are reminiscent of work by the Nabis (see page 102).

Gorky came from a Turkish Armenian family, as reflected in his mother's dress. He went to the United States in 1920.

20th-Century Sculpture

In the excitement of Cubist Paris, a number of sculptors were busy investigating ways to rethink three-dimensional art. A notable source of inspiration was the sculpture of Africa, which was shown in museums and exhibitions throughout Europe. The African sculptors behind such work showed little interest in copying reality—which, by contrast, had been the major concern of Western sculpture since ancient Greek times. Nonetheless, they created imaginative carvings of great power. Following this example, Western sculptors approached their work with a new freedom to apply their imagination. One trend was to simplify shapes; another was to bring entirely new materials to sculpture.

Right: Die *(1962) is a steel cube, 6 feet (1.8 m) in all directions, by the American Minimalist sculptor Tony Smith (1912–80).*

Minimalism
In the course of the 20th century, the trend to pare down artistic expression to a bare minimum gathered pace. Minimalism can be seen in architecture, music, painting, and particularly sculpture. The American Carl Andre (born 1935) famously produced a series of sculptures in 1966 called *Equivalents* that consist of nothing more than rectangular arrangements of industrial firebricks.

Henry Moore
The British sculptor Henry Moore (1898–1986) is celebrated for his public sculptures, in bronze or stone, that have a powerfully solid, monumental presence. Some of his work may seem abstract, but he almost always started from a real-life subject. With a reclining human figure, for instance, he would gradually break down and separate the shapes, and then inject spaces between them, ending with a composition that expressed only the essence of the original shape. The human form remained a constant inspiration to him, and even his very large sculptures retain a sense of humanity and tenderness. An exception to the rule might be his piece *Atomic Energy* (1967), a large bronze piece consisting of a massive ball on a rocklike tripod, but Moore said that even this was inspired by ancient sculpture of helmeted heads.

Above: Alexander Calder's Red Lily Pads *(1956) consists of 13 discs of painted sheet metal, carefully balanced on metal rods— and hanging over the atrium of the Guggenheim Museum in New York (see page 111).*

Hanging Mobiles
The American artist Alexander Calder (1898–1976) was living in Paris in the 1930s when he came across the experimental metal sculptures of Picasso and the Surrealist paintings of Joan Miró (see page 113). This inspired him to make metal sculptures that moved. In Russia, a group of abstract sculptors called the Constructivists had made clockwork-driven sculptures in the 1920s, but Calder decided that his sculptures would be driven only by the breeze. He created delicately balanced pieces consisting of cutout shapes of sheet metal, painted in primary colors or black and white, suspended from thin metal rods. Marcel Duchamp (see page 109) called these sculptures "mobiles"— the origin of the term now used generally for the hanging decorations often found in children's rooms.

Left: Family Group *(1945) was Henry Moore's first major commission after World War II. His tendency to simplify and exaggerate body shapes became even bolder in later years.*

Right: Man Pointing *(1947) is typical of Giacometti's emaciated bronze figures. However, standing about 6 feet (1.78 m) tall, it is relatively large. His figures are often much smaller.*

Alberto Giacometti

The Swiss sculptor Alberto Giacometti (1901–66) is celebrated for his powerfully expressive sculptures of wiry human figures, which he began to produce in 1947 while working in Paris. They are reminiscent of the stretched and elongated figures of some African wood sculpture but, instead of being smooth, Giacometti's cast-bronze figures have the rough texture of the fingered plaster and wire of his original models. The figures are also reminiscent of photographs of the emaciated survivors of the Nazi concentration camps, which had been liberated in 1945. Giacometti's sculptures, therefore, seem to speak of the frailty and vulnerability of the human race—of suffering as well as dignity.

Constantin Brancusi

Perhaps the greatest pioneer of modern sculpture, Constantin Brancusi (1876–1957) was born into a poor Romanian peasant family; in 1904 he walked to Paris. A naturally gifted sculptor, he could have become an assistant to Auguste Rodin (see page 99) but turned down the offer for fear of being overshadowed. Pursuing his own radical path, he began to pare down the shapes found in nature in search of the "essence of things," ending up with rounded forms that were virtually abstract and were the forerunners of Minimalism. His sculpture *Bird in Space* (1923) consists of a long, round, pointed, and polished piece of metal; in a famous incident, U.S. customs officals refused to allow it into New York, saying it was not art but just a lump of metal, for which import duty had to be paid.

Above: Brancusi's bronze sculpture Sleeping Muse *(c. 1906–10) depicts one of the Greek goddesses who inspire artists. It shows the clear influence of African sculpture.*

SHOWCASE: BOCCIONI, *UNIQUE FORMS OF CONTINUITY IN SPACE*

The Italian painter Umberto Boccioni (1882–1916) was a leading member of the Futurists, along with Giacomo Balla (see page 109). He was also a theorist of Futurist art, and the only sculptor of the group. In many ways, his sculpture expresses the key sentiments of Futurism: dynamism, energy, muscularity, machine-driven modernity, and a certain heartless brutality. His bronze figure *Unique Forms of Continuity in Space* is his most famous piece. It was exhibited as a clay model in 1913 and later cast in bronze. The Futurists welcomed war, but Boccioni was killed at age 33 in a riding accident while serving in the Italian army.

Boccioni believed that everything has "force lines," which explain their physical shape and presence. Here he shows the force lines extending from human muscles.

The polish of the bronze corresponds to the shiny qualities of machinery, which the Futurists so admired.

The influence of cubism can be seen in the interlocking flat surfaces.

The trailing flanges give the impression of wind and speed—a technique also used by Bernini (see page 69).

The rectangular blocks beneath the feet help to emphasize the dynamic curvature of the muscles.

Abstract Expressionism
Postwar Abstract Painting

For about 200 years, the center of art in the Western world was Paris. But after World War II, focus shifted to the United States, particularly New York. This is where the new trends in art were now being set, partly because the United States had emerged victorious and still prosperous after the war, and partly because in the 1930s and 1940s a large number of leading artists had fled Europe and settled in the United States. The first major new trend in art to emerge from the United States was Abstract Expressionism. One of the key pioneers was the American Jackson Pollock. He literally took paint and spattered it over large canvases, creating abstract paintings that directly expressed the emotions he felt at that time. In part, this was influenced by Surrealism: Pollock wanted to create art that was the direct product of his subconscious mind.

Mark Rothko
The Latvian-born American Mark Rothko (1903–70) was a leader in the kind of abstract Expressionism known as color field. Essentially, his paintings consist of large blocks of color painted onto a background. The blocks of color often have fuzzy, brushstroked edges, showing signs of painterly expression, but otherwise the viewer is left to respond to the paintings purely on the basis of the way that the colors and the shapes interact with each other. Rothko generally offered no clue to the meaning of his paintings, giving them titles such as *Orange*, *Brown*, and *Untitled*. However, he believed that his paintings convey strong human emotions and a sense of spirituality, and they have an impressive, glowing presence.

Above: This untitled painting from 1968, in acrylic on paper, is relatively small for a work by Rothko, just 17 inches (45 cm) wide.

Franz Kline
It was apparently when Franz Kline (1910–62) saw his drawings blown up to a large scale on a projector that he became inspired to create the kind of painting for which he became famous in the 1950 and 1960s. Painted with commercial house paints, and sometimes a wide house-painting brush, they look like hasty and spontaneous creations but were in fact carefully planned. Kline worked mainly in black and white—perhaps an echo of his childhood in the industrial coal-mining region of Pennsylvania. But he introduced vivid color into his work toward the end of his life.

Right: Elegy to the Spanish Republic, #131 *(1974) is one of more than 150 similar paintings relating to the Spanish Civil War by Robert Motherwell (1915–91), another leading American Abstract Expressionist.*

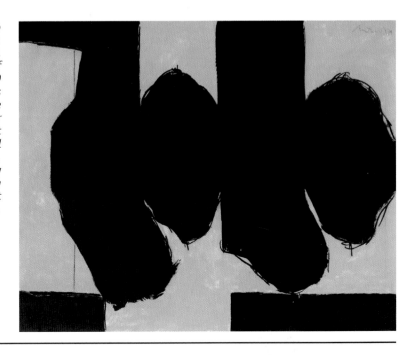

Above: Reminiscent of Chinese calligraphy, White Forms *(1955) is one of Kline's many black-and-white paintings. He worked on a large scale: The canvas is 6 feet 2 inches (1.89 m) wide.*

Frank Stella

In contrast to the Abstract Expressionists, the American painter Frank Stella (born 1936) wanted to reduce the traces of personal expression to a minimum, so that a picture became simply—as he put it—"a flat surface with paint on it." His series of "black pinstripe" paintings of 1959 consisted of nothing more than black canvases and numerous parallel lines. Later he started making shaped canvases, divided into brightly colored, geometric segments. His more recent work is far more expressive and colorful.

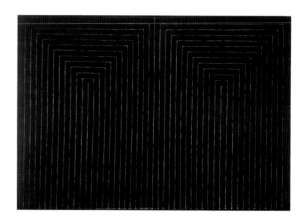

Above: Stella's "pinstripe" painting The Marriage of Reason and Squalor II *(1959) was made with commercial enamel paint, using a house-painter's brush. The title adds an element of mystery.*

Willem de Kooning

Dutch-born American Willem de Kooning (1904–97) arrived in the United States as a stowaway on a British freighter in 1926 and worked at first as a house painter. He went on to take a leading role in the development of Abstract Expressionism, and ranked alongside Jackson Pollock after World War II, producing his best work from 1950 to 1963. Always packed with vibrant energy and emotion, but with a delicate sense of color, de Kooning's paintings successfully strike a subtle balance between figurative and abstract art.

Above: Woman I *(1950–52) is de Kooning's most famous work; as the name suggests, it was part of a series of powerful semiabstract works depicting women.*

SHOWCASE: JACKSON POLLOCK, *NUMBER 1*

Jackson Pollock (1912–56) created his huge paintings by laying canvases on the floor. His work was hugely controversial: Critics complained that there was no talent involved in a painting like *Number 1* (1948)—anyone could do it. But that, in many ways, was precisely the point: Abstract Expressionism was hugely liberating. Pollock even used industrial paint, rather than the more expensive paint made specially for artists. His success, however, was short-lived: He died in a car accident in 1956 at the age of 44.

The abstract trails and blobs of paint are a record of the process of painting, which Pollock believed was as important as the finished work. This kind of art was later called Action Painting.

By eliminating manual brushstrokes Pollock created lines that crackle like surges of electricity.

Pollock dripped, dribbled, splashed, and slopped paint straight from the can. Chance played an important role in his art.

Roy Lichtenstein

The American painter Roy Lichtenstein (1923–97) made art out of comic strips. He created striking paintings based on the kind of pictures found in adult or adolescent comics, complete with speech bubbles—but he blew these up on a large scale. When he started doing this in the early 1960s, it was a deliberately provocative gesture: No one was expected to see comic strips as fine art. But in Lichtenstein's hand, the comic style did become something more weighty and interesting. His paintings made a big statement out of what would normally be just a single image in a story, turning it into something poignant, mysterious, funny, shocking, or just bizarre. Also, blown up large, the dots of pure color used in the color-printing process are very visible, giving the image an intriguing texture. Lichtenstein's work became instantly recognizable and hugely successful.

Right: In Drowning Girl *(1963), Lichtenstein finds absurd humor in a comic-strip moment of crisis.*

Pop Art and Op Art

To some artists, Abstract Expressionism was self-indulgent: It was all about the artist expressing his or her own emotions, and far too serious. Instead, they took a completely different path: Half-jokingly, they claimed to see art in commercial products—in advertisements, comics, and product labels, where there was no pretense of fine art and minimal signs of personal expression. Art, they argued, could be made simply by selecting and reproducing such items. The movement became known as Pop Art—because it was based on popular culture and consumer products. Although some argue that the first stirrings occurred in Britain, pop art was essentially an American phenomenon.

Jasper Johns

In the 1950s, before Pop Art had really begun in the United States, the American artist Jasper Johns (born 1930) had begun making paintings based on commercial products and popular images of American culture. He used oil paints on canvas in a traditional style, with painterly brushwork, but his subjects were highly unconventional, such as simple targets (1955) and the American flag (1957). Both Johns and fellow American Robert Rauschenberg (born 1925) took an irreverent attitude toward art and were sometimes called Neo-Dadaist (see page 112). Rauschenberg's most notorious work was a sculpture called *Monogram* (1959), which consisted of a stuffed long-haired goat splashed with paint, and with a tire around its middle. Pop Art aimed to depersonalize art. The work of Johns and Rauschenberg, by contrast, is more individualistic.

Below: Numbers in Color *(1958) is exactly what its title says, but Jasper Johns pushes these common symbols past the point of recognizability.*

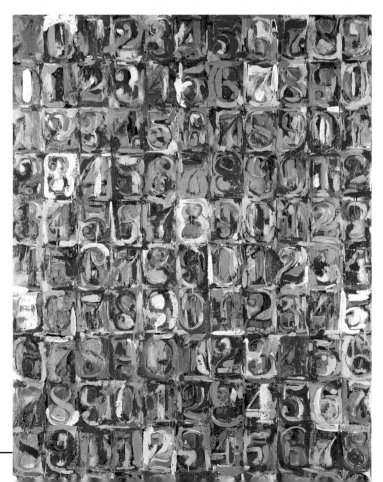

Andy Warhol

The most famous of all the Pop Artists was Andy Warhol (1928–87), an American born to Czech parents in Pittsburgh. He started his career as a successful commercial artist making advertisements, but in the early 1960s his literal copies of consumer products, treated as art, caused a sensation. He set up a "factory" to mass-produce silk-screen prints and developed a cult as an art celebrity. He seemed to be amused at the way he could turn commercial art into fine art and make that glamorous.

Left: One of Andy Warhol's most famous series depicted Campbell's Soup cans, which he reproduced numerous times as silk-screen prints.

Op Art

Tricks of the eye, or optical illusions, have always been a source of fascination, and trompe l'oeil painting has played a role in art since Roman times. In the 1930s, the Hungarian-born artist Victor Vasarely (1908–97) began to produce abstract paintings that used clashing colors and webs of lines that confuse the eye. By the 1960s, he had become famous for this work, and other younger artists pursued the same goal. Among them was the British artist Bridget Riley (born 1931). This was the era of Pop Art—so optical work was jokingly labeled Op Art. Their paintings also had something in common with Pop Art in that they tended to be produced with almost mechanical perfection to maximize the confusion to the eye. Some large op art paintings seem to move, throb, and vibrate, and make the eyes swim—but others can be soothing.

Below: The way that the dots change shape toward the middle in Bridget Riley's Fission *(1963) suggests perhaps two rollers, but the image is complicated by the slight kink at the center.*

Above: James Rosenquist's F-111 *(1964–65) is a huge painting consisting of 23 sections, designed to fill four walls of a room. The glossy images include a smiling girl sitting under a hair dryer (which looks a bit like a bomb), laid over an F-111 American bomber aircraft.*

Consumer Art

A forerunner of American Pop Art was the British artist Richard Hamilton (born 1922), who in 1956 produced what may have been the first Pop Art work: an amusing collage containing various cutout images of consumer products called *Just What Is It That Makes Today's Homes So Different, So Appealing?* When Hamilton said that he wanted to produce art that was "popular, transient, expendable, low cost, mass produced, young, witty, sexy, gimmicky, glamorous, and big business," he more or less summed up the Pop Art agenda. The American Pop Artist James Rosenquist (born 1933) started his career in the 1950s as a commercial billboard painter and went on to produce very large, posterlike paintings of glossy, overlapping consumer products, often in startling combinations.

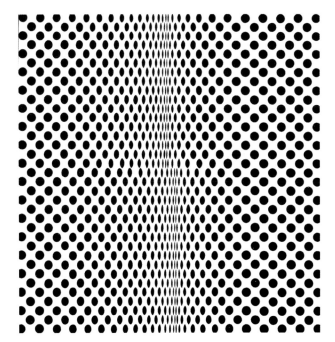

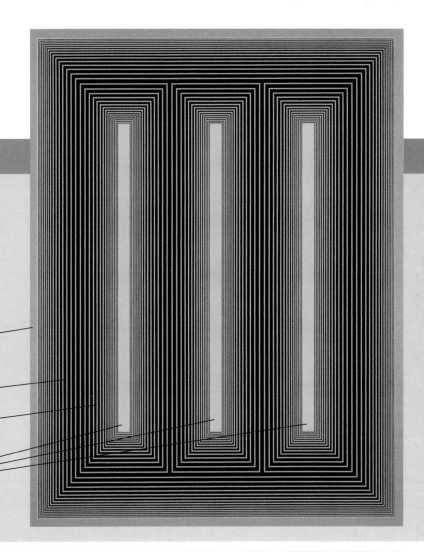

SHOWCASE: ANUSZKIEWICZ, *TEMPLE OF RADIANT YELLOW*

Richard Anuszkiewicz (born 1930) is a major force in Op Art. Born in Pennsylvania, he trained with the German artist and teacher Josef Albers (1888–1926), who was famous for his long series of abstract paintings featuring squares. The work of Anuszkiewicz typically focuses on rectangular forms, as seen in *Temple of Radiant Yellow* (1985). Anuszkiewicz first made his mark in 1965, when he took part in the exhibition at the Museum of Modern Art in New York called "The Responsive Eye," which effectively launched Op Art onto the world stage.

The pale-blue border on all sides provides a contrasting foreground of cool tonality that helps to detach the hot yellows from the surface of the painting.

The lines are drawn with clean-edged precision. Their regularity is soothing.

The spacing between the lines narrows, creating a tunnel-like effect. The painting looks three-dimensional.

The three long strips of yellow radiate light— in a manner that seems almost spiritual, as the painting's title suggests.

New Media
New Directions

One hundred years ago, art was made by putting oil paint on canvas or sculpting in marble and bronze. There were a few other alternatives, but not many. Then—around 1911–13—came Picasso and Marcel Duchamp with their art composed of ready-made or found objects, and suddenly the possibilities were wide open. Since that time, Western art has been transformed. In the 1950s, some artists, such as the German Joseph Beuys (1921–86), gave performances as their form of artistic expression. In the 1960s, the American Minimalist artist Dan Flavin (1933–96) produced installations using neon light strips. In the 1990s, the British artist Damien Hirst (born 1965) made vitrines of real dead animals preserved in glass tanks. In other words, these days artistic ideas can be expressed through any means that seem appropriate.

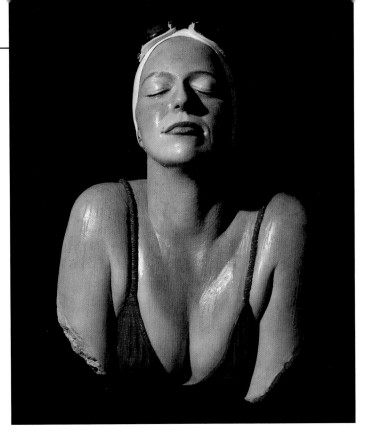

Above: Grande Catalina *(2005) is one of a number of Hyperrealist sculptures of female swimmers made from painted resin by Carole Feuerman.*

Hyperrealism
There is Realism, and then there is Hyperrealism—realism that is so much like real life that a painting looks like a photograph and a sculpture looks like a real person. The effect can be unsettling. The American painter Chuck Close (born 1940) is the master of the outsized Hyperrealistic portrait, with every detail painted with photographic precision, down to the last eyelash. This kind of precision-imitation can be even more disturbing in three dimensions. The Australian sculptor Ron Mueck (born 1958), who trained as a model-maker and puppeteer for film, creates seemingly real replicas (in fiberglass, silicone, and resin) of human beings in all their imperfections, but at the wrong scale—either much larger or much smaller. A number of American sculptors have also become well known for their Hyperrealist work, including Duane Hanson (1925–96), who made casts directly from his living models, and Carole Feuerman (born 1945).

Photography
The potential of photography as an art form was recognized soon after its invention in the 1830s, but it has joined the mainstream of gallery art only relatively recently. A number of contemporary artists have used photography as their main means of expression. The American Cindy Sherman (born 1954) makes scripted portraits of herself, commenting wryly on the stereotyped roles of women in society. The British duo Gilbert and George (Gilbert Proesch, born 1943; George Passmore, born 1942) use photographs, often of themselves, to make large, provocative pieces that are reminiscent of stained glass.

Below: The Korean American Nam June Paik (1932–2006) was one of the pioneers of video art. In this installation from his exhibition at the Museum of Modern Art in New York in 1977, a Buddha statue gazes fixedly at its own projected image.

Above: In 1977–80, Cindy Sherman made a series of 69 self-portraits called Untitled Film Stills, *imitating the sorts of images that came from B movies and European art films.*

Video
Art is about images and ideas, and a supreme modern image-maker is the video camera. It is particularly useful to artists because it is light, portable, relatively cheap, and capable of creating intimate and personal records that correspond to an artist's individual vision. Video art can explore the world and the imagination in a different way from cinema or television film because it does not have to win the attention of a commercial audience. The American Bill Viola (born 1951) has made a great variety of pieces, often dealing with the big issues of human existence, such as intense emotion, birth, death, and grief.

Above: The American Robert Smithson (1938–73) was a pioneer of land art. He made Spiral Jetty *in the Great Salt Lake, Utah, in 1970, using 6,550 tons of rock and earth.*

Earth Art

"Non-gallery" art—work that cannot be put in a gallery—became a feature of late-20th-century art. Earth art (or land art) is an extreme example of this: It involves artists making changes to the landscape, sometimes on a grand scale. Walter de Maria (born 1935), an American artist and composer, made a giant piece called *Lightning Field* (1977) consisting of 400 steel poles set out in a grid measuring about half a mile (800 m) by 1 mile (1.6 km), in New Mexico. The British artist Richard Long (born 1945) records, maps, and photographs walks that he takes across landscapes, and creates sculptures from the rocks he has found along the way.

Installations

The term *sculpture* has proved quite inadequate to describe the kind of three-dimensional, mixed-media work produced by artists since the 1950s. At first such pieces were called "assemblages," and now "installations." There is limitless variety in this field: Some installations are vast and fill landscapes; others are tiny. The British artist Cornelia Parker (born 1956) made her *Cold Dark Matter: An Exploded View* (1991) by blowing up a wooden shed filled with household objects and then hanging the shattered remains from the gallery ceiling in a gridlike block. The American artist Jeff Koons (born 1955) makes Pop Art–style pieces in all kinds of media: His huge *Puppy* (1997), installed outside the Guggenheim Museum in Bilbao, Spain, was coated in 70,000 flowering plants.

Above: American artists Christo and Jeanne-Claude (both born 1935) take textiles into landscapes, as in The Gates, Central Park, New York City, 1979–2005. *Photo by Wolfgang Volz © Christo and Jeanne-Claude 2005.*

SHOWCASE: HOCKNEY, *PEARBLOSSOM HIGHWAY, 11–18 APRIL 1986, #1*

The British artist David Hockney (born 1937) is one of the best-known modern painters, famous for his distinctive vision and his deliberately stylized or naive imagery and a color range of pastel-softness. In the 1980s, however, he began making collages using photographs taken on the spot with a Polaroid instant camera. *Pearblossom Highway, 11–18 April 1986, #1* is one of two similar pieces made on a journey along California State Route 138. It consists of some 750 individual color photographs.

With their varying color tones, the overlapping photographs give a painterly effect, noticeable, for instance, in the sky.

The yucca trees recall the spindly palm trees Hockney used in his famous Californian paintings, such as *A Bigger Splash* (1967).

Pearblossom Highway seems an ironic title, given this desert scene. The name comes from the town called Pearblossom on the route.

The roadside garbage points to the notion that the awesome beauty of the desert has been desecrated by human activity, including the road itself and the signposts.

The slightly misplaced lettering helps to remind the viewer that this is an artistic interpretation, not a precise photographic record.

Hockney said that the landscape has two viewpoints: The signposts on the right are the driver's perspective of the route, while the passenger is free to look at the landscape on the left.

Index

Numbers in **bold** refer to illustrations

Acknowledgments

All efforts have been made to obtain and provide compensation for the copyright to the photos and artworks in this book in accordance with legal provisions. Persons who may nevertheless still have claims are requested to contact the copyright owners.

The publishers would like to thank the following archives, museums, photographers, and institutions and artists who have authorized the reproduction of the works in this book:

t=top; tl=top left; tc=top center; tr=top right; c=center; cl=center left; cr=center right; b=bottom; bl=bottom left; bc=bottom center; br=bottom right

Art Resource, New York: © Vanni/Art Resource, NY: 19br

Artothek: 63tl

Bridgeman Art Library, London: cover c, 7t, 7cr, 8tr, 8cl, 9br, 10cr, 10br, 11cr, 12tl, 12bl, 13tr, 13bl, 13bc, 13br, 14cl, 14br, 17cr, 19bl, 21bl, 21br, 24tr, 28cr, 30tl, 30br, 32tr, 32cl, 33cr, 33b, 35tl, 40tl, 41tr, 43tr, 46bl, 49tc, 51bl, 53br, 54tl, 54tr, 55cl, 55cr, 55bc, 56tl, 61tl, 61tr, 62tl, 63cr, 63bl, 64tl, 64tr, 65tl, 65tr, 66tr, 66cr, 68tc, 68tr, 71cl, 72cl, 74tl, 76b, 77tl, 77b, 78cr, 79tl, 79tr, 79b, 81tr, 83tr, 84tr, 84cl, 84cr, 85cr, 86cr, 87b, 88tr, 88cl, 88br, 89t, 89cr, 90tr, 90cl, 90br, 91tr, 91b, 92tr, 92cl, 92cr, 94t, 95t, 95bl, 95br, 96br, 97bl, 98tl, 98cr, 98bl, 99tl, 99 tr, 99br, 100cl, 101tl, 101tr, 102tr, 102b, 103tl, 103bl, 106cl, 107cl, 112b, 115bl, 117bl, 118br, 120br

Corbis: © Adam Woolfitt/Corbis 7bl; © The Art Archive/Corbis 9cr; © Vanni Archive/Corbis 17br; © Ladislav Janicek/zefa/Corbis 23bl; © Atlantide Phototravel/Corbis 24tl; © Francis G. Mayer/Corbis 26cl; © Krause, Johansen/Archivo Iconografico, SA/Corbis 36br; © Archivo Iconografico, S.A./Corbis 65b; © Michael S. Yamashita/Corbis 71br; © Brian A. Vikander/Corbis 72br; © Andrea Jemolo/Corbis 73tr; © Werner Forman/Corbis 73br; © Historical Picture Archive/Corbis 76tr; © Massimo Listri/Corbis 80tr; © Francis G. Mayer/Corbis 114tr; © Scott Smith/Corbis 123tl

Cameraphoto Arte, Venice: 29br, 34tl, 70bl

© **Carole Feuerman:** 122tr

Collection of Dr and Dr Bryan Ho: © 1985 by Richard Anuszkiewicz, 121br

© **David Hockney:** 123b

© **The Hirschsprung Collection, Copenhagen:** 87tl

LAIF/Contrasto, Milan: Photo by Wolfgang Volz, © 2005 by Christo and Jeanne-Claude, 123tr.

Erich Lessing/Contrasto, Milan: 20tr, 22cl, 27bl, 31tl, 72tr, 81b, 93br

The Metropolitan Museum of Art, New York: Gift of J. Pierpont Morgan, 1917 (17.190.396) Photograph © 2000 The Metropolitan Museum of Art 29tr; H.O. Havemeyer Collection, Bequest of Mrs. H.O. Havemeyer, 1929 (29.100.129) Photograph © 1991 The Metropolitan Museum of Art 87tr,

The National Gallery, London: 52tr, 76tl

Rijksmuseum, Amsterdam: 62cr

Photo RMN, Paris: © Hervé Lewandowski 20bc, © Martine Beck-Coppola 73cl, © Béatrice Hatala 105tr

© **Foto Scala, Florence:** cover l, cover r, 6cl, 9cl, 9bl, 11tr, 12cr, 14tr, 15 tl, 15tc, 15tr, 15b, 17cl, 18tl, 18tc, 18tr, 18cr, 19tl, 19tr, 20cl, 21c, 22br, 23t, 23cr, 24cr, 25tl, 25tr, 26tl, 26cr, 27tl, 28tl, 29cl, 29bl, 30tr, 31bl, 33tl, 34bl, 35tr, 36tl, 36cr, 37tr, 37cl, 37br, 38tl, 38tr, 38br, 39tr, 39cl, 39br, 40tr, 40cr, 40bl, 41b, 42bl, 43cl, 44tl, 44br, 45c, 46tl, 46cr, 47tl, 47tr, 47bl, 48c, 48br, 49cl, 49cr, 49br, 50tl, 50br, 51tc, 52cl, 53tr, 53cl, 54br, 56tr, 56cr, 57tl, 57tr, 57br, 58tl, 58tr, 58b, 59tr, 59c, 59br, 60tl, 62br, 63tr, 64cr, 67t, 67bl, 67br, 68c, 68bl, 68br, 69tl, 69tc, 69br, 70tr, 70br, 71tr, 74tr, 74cr, 75tr, 75b, 77tr, 80c, 80b, 82tr, 82br, 83tl, 83b, 85b, 86tl, 86tr, 89bl, 93t, 93bl, 94cl, 94br, 96tr, 96cl, 97tl, 97c, 100tr, 100br, 101b, 102cr, 103cr, 104tl, 104tr, 104cr, 105tl, 105b, 106tr, 107tl, 107cr, 108tr, 108bl, 108br, 109tr, 112t, 113tl, 113c, 113bl, 114cl, 114br, 115tl, 116tr, 116br, 117c, 117br, 118tr, 118cl, 119tl, 119tr, 119br, 120tr, 120bl, 121tr, 121cl, courtesy the artist and Metro Pictures 122cl, 122br; © Austrian Archive/Scala, Florence: 61cl; © Scala, Florence/Bildarchiv Preussischer Kulturbesitz: 78bl, 82bl; © Werner Forman Archive/Scala, Florence : 32bl; © The Philadelphia Museum of Art/Art Resource/Scala, Florence: 85tl, 109tl; © Scala, Florence — with permission of Ministro Beni e Attività Culturali: 22tr, 22cl, 42tr, 44tr, 45bl, 45br, 51bl, 66tl, 75tl, 81tl; © Scala, Florence/HIP: 78tl, 91tl; © Spectrum/HIP/Scala, Florence: 15tr, 16cl, 25cr, 31br, 110tr, 110c, 110bl, 110br, 111cl; **Solomon R. Guggenheim Museum, New York:** 106br; 109b; photograph by David Heald © The Solomon R. Guggenheim Foundation, New York 116cl

The Trustees of the Wallace Collection, London: 60bl

The Vatican Museums: 52br

Wadsworth Atheneum Museum of Art, Hartford, CT. The Ella Gallup Sumner and Mary Catlin Sumner Collection Fund: 60tr

Whitney Museum of American Art, Gift of Julian Levy for Maro and Natasha Gorky: 115cr

Illustrations by: Lorenzo Cecchi; Matteo Chesi; MM Comunicazione (Mauela Cappon, M. Favilli); Studio Stalio (Ivan Stalio, Fabiano Fabbrucci); Tiziano Perotto; Paola Ravaglia; Andrea Ricciardi di Gaudesi.